ON THE SHORE
SEASIDE LIVING

The Deutsche Nationalbibliothek lists this publication in the Deutsche Nationalbibliografie; detailed bibliographic data are available on the Internet at http://dnb.dnb.de

ISBN 978-3-03768-213-5

www.braun-publishing.ch

1st edition 2017

Project coordination: Editorial office van Uffelen
Editor: Anne-Sophie Müller, Lisa Rogers, Johanna Schröder
Graphic concept: Michaela Prinz, Berlin
Reproduction: Bild1Druck GmbH, Berlin

ON THE SHORE
SEASIDE LIVING

Markus Sebastian Braun

BRAUN

CONTENT

PREFACE

It's all about the view! Anyone who builds a house on the coast wants views over the water and that's why the massive windows are often one of the most important characteristics of the design; a dematerialized wall with glass panes that can be opened out wide so that the ocean is not only visually observed but also experienced as a sound, a smell and a feeling carried into the living space on the wind. The houses presented in "Seaside Living" protect their inhabitants from the breaking waves but life is nevertheless oriented towards the horizon. The imperturbable here and now of the building becomes the anchor point for the sweeping views that are as reliable as the tides that flow in and ebb out, bringing ships closer and then drawing them into the distance again; or the seagulls that tumble in the wind; the storms that come and go and the sun that will rise and then set once more. The story told of a day by the sea will always be dominated by the view that characterizes the living space. The buildings are often open on more than one side. The side facing the land is rather plain in order to camouflage the dwelling's main purpose – a refuge of quiet retreat embedded into the landscape.

The façade is not intended to draw admiring glances from those passing by, the design itself is dedicated to the views of the sea, in keeping with the requirement that function is of greater importance than form. The architecture is not slave to a theoretical stylistic demand, it is slave to the view and the desire for uninterrupted views of the crashing waves and the horizon beyond. The floor plans also don't necessarily follow the path of the sun as it moves through the sky during the day, they more often follow the water's edge, determined by the usually sloping terrain. The less important rooms are often located on the landside, while the rooms where the most time is spent are organized to make the most of the view.

Some of the sloping sites also offer the opportunity to double this organization; so that the areas facing the landside can have views of the sea over the 'heads' of the water-facing rooms. In this case it is not only the master bedroom that can enjoy the striking landscape and the rolling waves. Large open spaces between the house and the sea are often independent spaces in themselves, uniting two incompatible worlds. Gardens are seldom part of the design as these would just block the views of the water or distract the observer. Far-reaching swimming pools and sun decks, long wood or stone terraces take priority and boast clear lines that are reminiscent of the horizon itself. In terms of style, the buildings in this volume are extremely modern. The windows are large out of necessity and this demands a modern and technically sophisticated construction. The wide windows demand a robust concrete structure, either painted white or left as exposed concrete. Natural materials are also often used and seek to establish a connection between the inhabitants and their surroundings. They also help to embed the building into the context without spoiling the natural beauty of the site. Other materials such as stone walls, wood cladding or natural stone facing also help to accentuate the building, emphasizing the fact that it is indeed a building, an architectural edifice in its own right. These houses are the work of man, built to protect the inhabitants from the forces of nature and transforming the surrounding nature into a never-ending panorama.

A little like an eagle's nest perched on the lofty heights of the cliffs, above the tumultuous surf that observes the timelessness of the water and fulfills our inner longing for the sensuality of the past and a glimpse of the future.

HOUSE ON THE CLIFF
GRANADA, SPAIN

The construction of the House on the Cliff relied heavily on craftsmanship and local labor. The house was to be built during Spain's worst possible financial crisis, with an unemployment rate of almost 36 percent in the region where the house was built. Within this social context the architects decided to avoid machine-made industrial construction systems and develop an architecture that is based on many hours of labor.

The most complex elements of the house demonstrate this approach: For example, the reinforced concrete structure of the roof is based on a manually executed metal formwork; the roof tiles are handmade; the interior bespoke furniture was made with fiberglass and polyester resin and was designed by using digital design software, but manufactured by hand on-site. The roof was created using a handcrafted formwork system developed by a local engineer, using a very efficient deformable metal mesh. This technique was manufactured at a much lower cost in comparison to the options that are commonly used in construction such as timber or steel formworks. The surface of the roof comprises zinc scales that were laid and fabricated by hand from raw material. Another important feature is the roof's double curved concrete shell with 40 centimeters of insulation that serves as the formwork for the concrete of the upper shell.

Architect/designer: Pablo Gil and Jaime Bartolomé GilBartolomé Architects
Local engineer: Dr. Manuel Rojas
Year of completion: 2015
No. of rooms: 3 bedrooms
Gross floor area/site area: 247 m^2/720m^2
Luxury features : swimming pool

In terms of energy performance, the house is embedded in the ground and the architects have managed to turn this to their advantage as the ground temperature is a constant 19.5 degrees throughout the year. Between the interior and the retaining walls there is a 40-centimeter air cavity that is used to regulate the amount of warm air that enters the house, to determine how much goes into the pre-cooling or pre-heating of the HVAC system, and how much has to be ventilated in order to control the humidity levels.

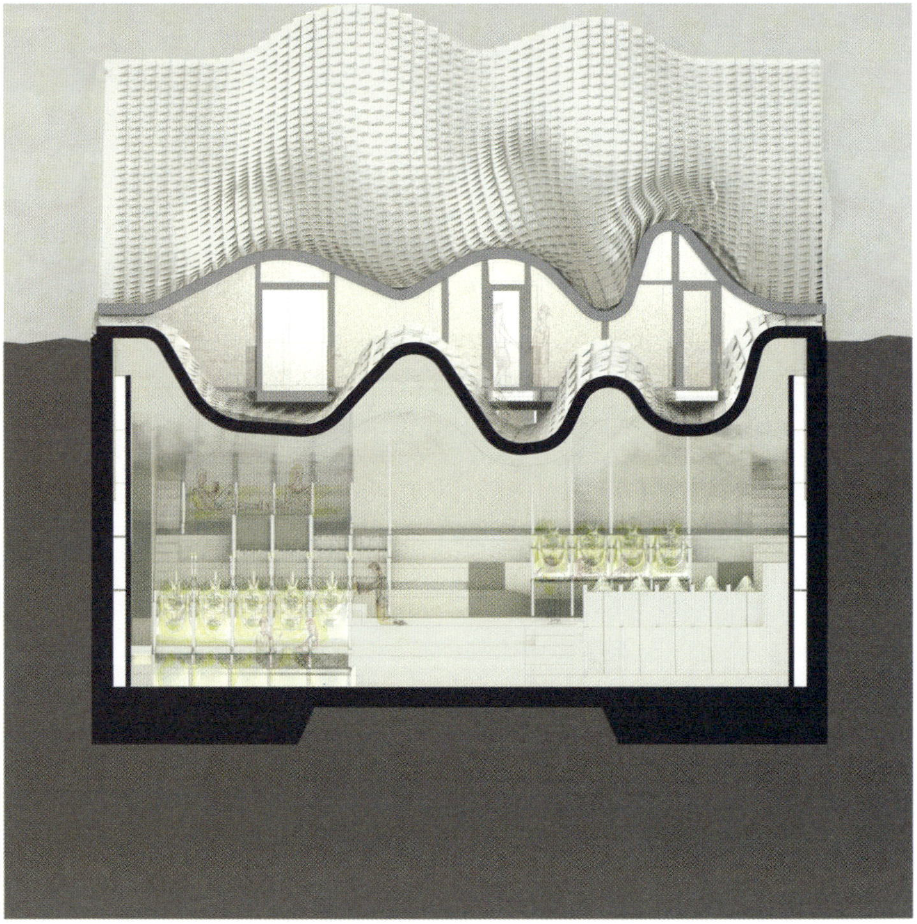

An undulating shell embedded into the cliffs, just open it to see if there's a pearl inside.

Over 40 years ago, a couple purchased a 1,000 square meters of land located 150 meters from the Atlantic Ocean. When the state, county, and town codes evolved, everything that was purchased as a buildable lot had to undergo extensive negotiations to permit even the smallest house. 56 square meters was the largest house that could be built. Subtle shifts in the geometry of the building section maximize natural light and views to the sky, expanding the perception of space and openness while maintaining the required footprint. As the walls splay out from the base of the building toward the roof, the resulting void is a central light well. The bedroom and study are separated by clear glass walls on either side of the light well, but appear to be one large space. The acoustically divided rooms can be made more private by lowering the privacy shades. To address the restricted height requirements, the floor and roof plates are engineered to be as thin as possible. Traditional ductwork is eliminated from the floors and roof and each space employs a separate individually controlled mechanical unit yielding higher energy efficiency.

BEACH HAMPTON
AMAGANSETT, NY, USA

Architect: Bates Masi + Architects
Year of completion: 2014
No. of rooms: 2
Gross floor area/site area: 56 m²/1,113 m²

This unique way of addressing each space is a study in sustainability relating to build smaller and living with less. Part of the approval process included a required raised portion of the site dedicated to storm water control and sanitary system. This portion of the engineering requirement was utilized by treating the raised area as the foreground to the architecture. The plinth is landscaped with a native grass that captures the patterns of the wind and references the nearby ocean waves. Located at the end of the path through the grass, the house is an object in the landscape perched on the edge of the plinth.

Less is more does not mean less luxurious.

Situated on a cliff site overlooking the Atlantic Ocean, Cliff House in Dakar, Senegal was completed in 2011. The house was designed for a Senegalese businessman and his family. Built on the site of an old World War II bunker and on the edge of a cliff, Cliff House maximizes its commanding position to create a house that is not only dramatic but with the incorporation of historical elements quite magical and mysterious. Part of the old bunker has been retained and a portion of it now houses an underground cinema that opens up into a water courtyard and a moat that runs along the boundary creating a water feature at the gateway to the property. The living and dining spaces cantilever over the cliff and hang over the ocean, enjoying panoramic sea views as well as views back to the house. The kitchen made up of a so-called 'American' or open kitchen and a separate traditional kitchen as well as the garage and staff facilities run along the east-west axis and along the northern side of the boundary.

CLIFF HOUSE
DAKAR, SENEGAL

Architect: SAOTA
Interior designer: ARRCC
Furniture supplier: OKHA Interiors
Year of completion: 2011
Site area: 1,954 m²
Luxury features: swimming pool, cinema

One of the features of the house is the spiral staircase, clad in stainless steel, while the treads are clad in white granite. To add to the sense of continuity between the levels, the stainless steel rods run from the first floor handrail to the lower ground floor, thus making the stairwell look like a sculptural steel cylinder.

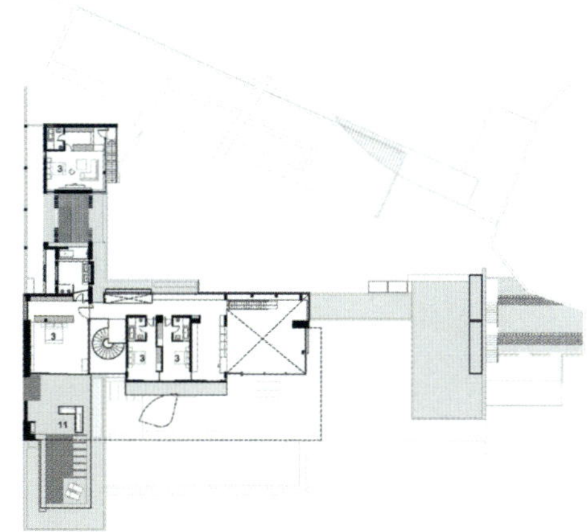

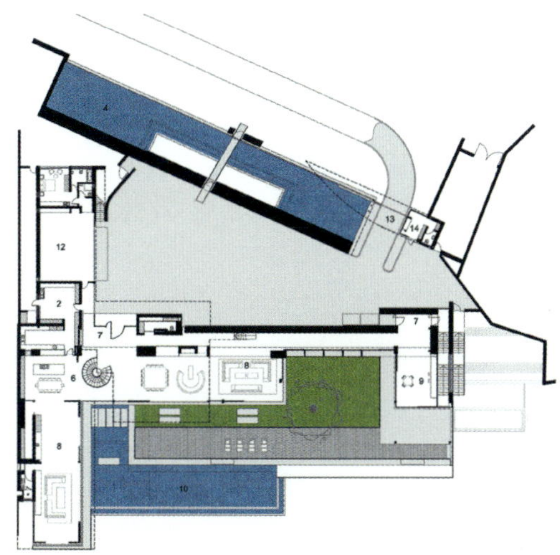

The infinity pool almost appears to flow into the ocean, the perfect place to gaze at the sea and to contemplate the horizon.

The Dune House, half-sunk into the dunes on the northern coast of the island of Terschelling, rises over the landscape and looks over the dunes providing a breath-taking view of the North Sea. The sea, the sunlight and the local wind patterns have had a profound effect on the design, which almost looks as if it has been sculpted by the elements. It is above all a very contextual design and for this reason every material was chosen with careful consideration of the colors and textures found in the environment. This results in a peculiar architectonic object, a wooden diamond that is experienced very differently from each of its sides, it is fully integrated into the landscape and yet also makes a strong but subtle connection between its interior and its immediate surroundings. The interior of the house reflects the experience of going for a walk on the dunes. Inside, a spiraling route winds around the core as a continuous path leading from platform to platform, each just a few steps higher than the next. This generates interesting spatial and visual relationships between the various rooms.

DUNE HOUSE
TERSCHELLING, THE NETHERLANDS

Architect/designer: Marc Koehler Architects
Interior designer: Marc Koehler Architects
Year of completion: 2014
No. of rooms: 10
Gross floor area: 180 m²

The design takes care to respect the stunning location, and this is reflected by the construction method using prefabricated wooden panels, designed using BIM (Building Information Management) software, which drastically reduced the building time and the impact on the site. The intensive use of wood, the implementation of passive methods to avoid unwanted heat gain and loss, combined with the use of solar panels to generate energy and a biomass-fueled fireplace make this a very environmentally friendly design with a minimal ecological footprint.

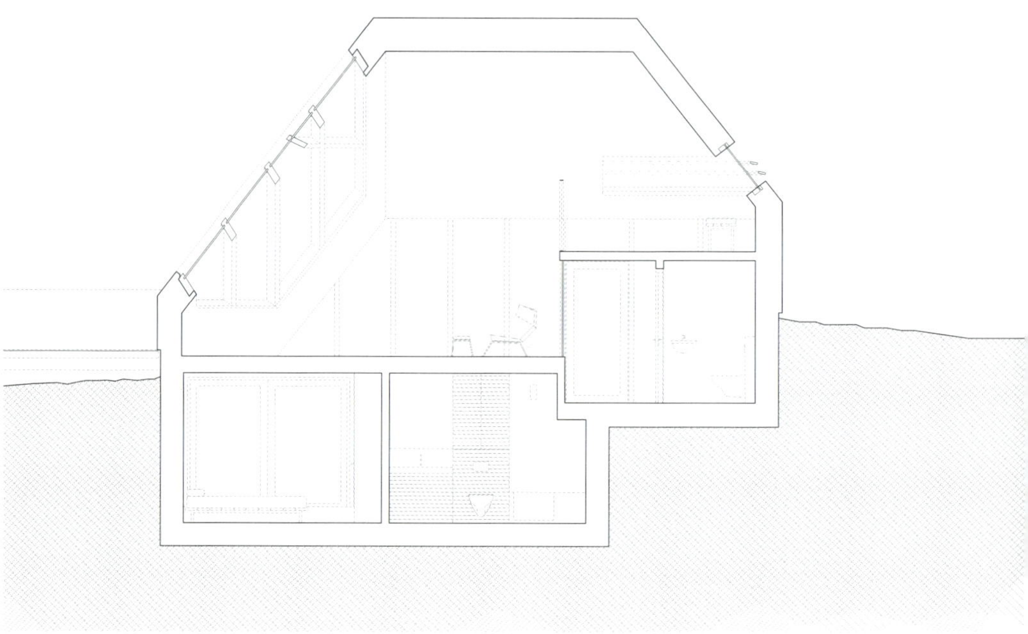

The architecture is reminiscent of a shifting dune that is shaped by the direction of the wind.

This project was conceived as a collection of accrued simple shed-like dwellings in an isolated and south-facing New Zealand coastal surf community. The design strategy comprised the construction of a sequence of sets of buildings. These new 'shed' sets are then offset to allow seasonal living, provide circulation and various privacy options as well as variations in wind and sun exposure. During the summer months, the 'sheds' are open and inviting, welcoming the community; with diagonal movement connecting offset and shaded external spaces. During the summer, the amount of time spent inside is minimal, with summer circulation defining informal house boundaries. During the winter, more time is spent inside, with high level northern openings capturing precious northern light and warmth, while offset forms provide shelter to the southern exposure. The 'shed' typology follows New Zealand architectural vernacular accruing from rural and isolated beginnings, and the simple, self erected, elemental buildings which are still apparent within these remote provincial communities.

OFFSET SHED HOUSE
GISBORNE, NEW ZEALAND

Architect: Irving Smith Architects
Interior designer: Irving Smith Architects
Year of completion: 2013
No. of rooms: 7
Gross floor area/site area: 145 m²/809 m²

Within this new set of 'sheds', timber pergolas and ceilings collate pathways within simple metal and plasterboard linings to efficiently define offset spaces and welcome an eclectic collection of furniture, the coastal community, and surf. The simplicity of the construction is also reflected by the interior design, which is a mixture of wood, white walls, and simple yet elegant furnishings.

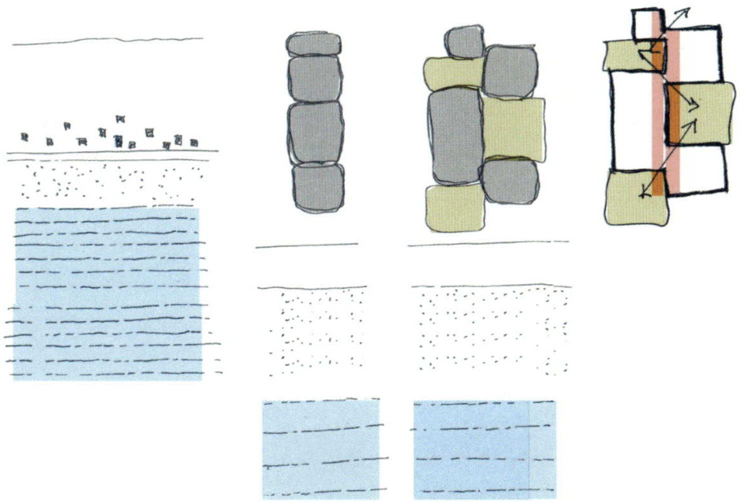

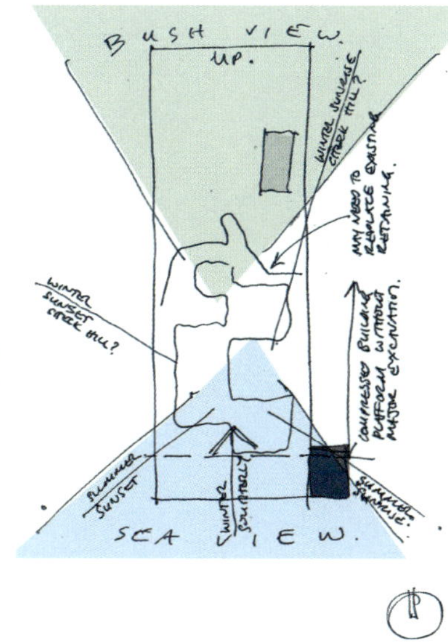
BUSH VIEW.
UP.
WINTER SUNRISE CHECK HILL?
MAY NEED TO REPLACE EXISTING RETAINING.
WINTER SUNSET CHECK HILL?
COMPRESSED BUILDING PLATFORM WITHOUT MAJOR EXCAVATION.
SUMMER SUNSET
SUMMER SUNRISE.
SEA VIEW.

Live your life without boundaries in your mind and in your house.

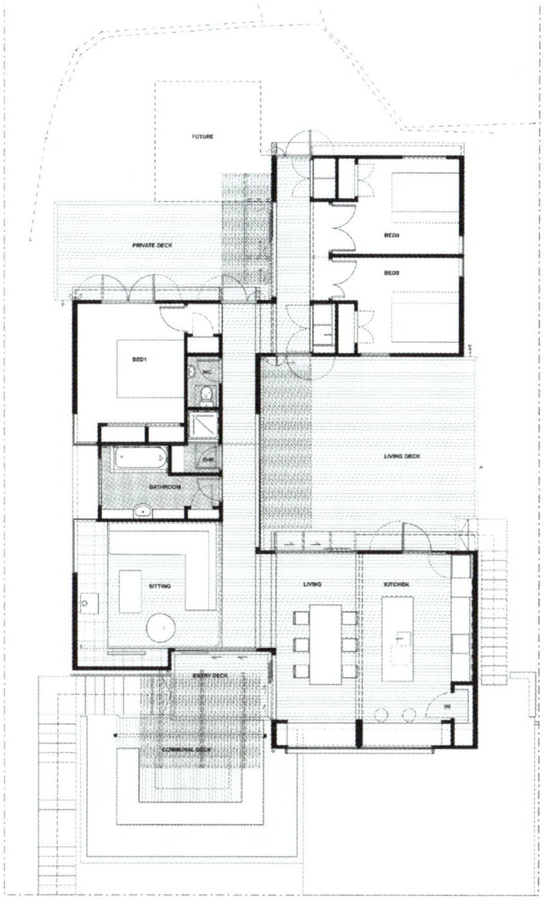
FUTURE
PRIVATE DECK
BED3
BED2
BED1
WC
SHR
BATHROOM
LIVING DECK
SITTING
LIVING
KITCHEN
ENTRY DECK
COMMUNAL DECK

This ocean-front residence captures a sense of indoor-outdoor living by introducing large cantilevered decks and roof decks. Designed for an active family who loves to cook and entertain, the ability to do so on each level is a driving element. As a measure to preserve the integrity of the dune, the house is pulled back from it to create three distinct experiences on each level. The ground level is nestled behind the dune and provides a mixed wood and concrete paved patio with a pool, outdoor fireplace and covered ping-pong area. Areas on this level intended for storage and lower level entry are enclosed by a combination of glass and concrete walls. The main floor is accessed from an exterior cantilevered stair that leads to the central light-filled atrium. This main level houses all the bedrooms and a centrally located family room.

OCEAN DECK HOUSE
BRIDGEHAMPTON, NY, USA

Architect: Stelle Lomont Rouhani Architects
Landscape architect: Edmund Hollander Design
Year of completion: 2014
No. of rooms: 11
Gross floor area/site area: 866 m²/5,354 m²

This house is designed as an upside down house, giving the most spectacular views to the living room, dining area and kitchen on the top floor. The large windows not only break up the solidity of the volume, they also make the most views of the ocean, the pool and the surroundings. This floor takes advantage not only of the southern exposure and views, but provides for adequate solar control. The main terrace reaches out towards the sea and is large enough to easily accommodate a huge table, sofas, chairs and a fireplace. It also allows for an extensive herb and vegetable garden, making it the perfect place for outdoor cooking, entertaining and lounging.

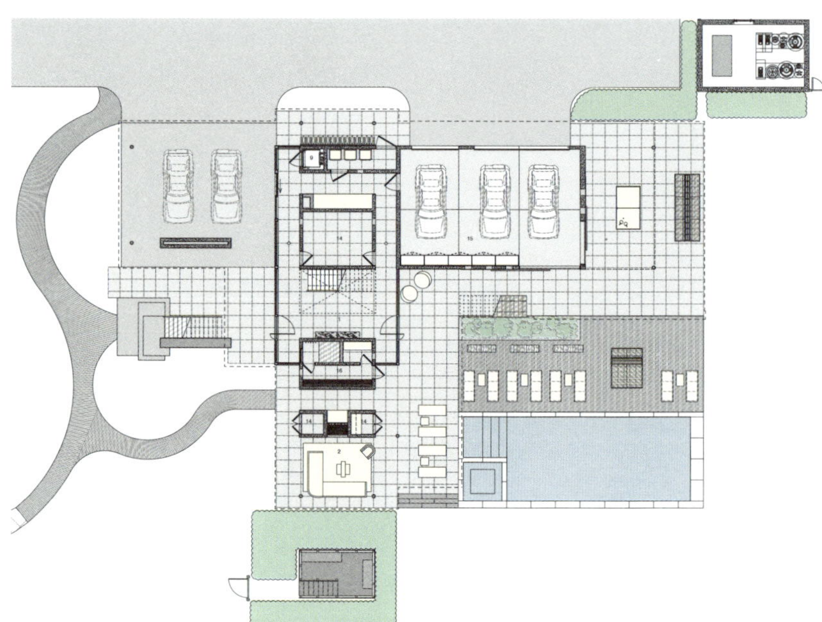

Natural colors give the house an elegant and bright esthetic, welcoming you inside.

Nestled behind the dunes, this house is designed to take advantage of the spectacular site while being sensitive to the natural landscape surrounding it. Conceived as two offset stacked boxes, the first floor steps away from the landscape creating a private outdoor sitting area that is defined by both the cantilevered volume above and the dunes. Three guest bedrooms with adjacent bathrooms, a large media room and building services make up the lower level. The bedrooms, while modest in size, all have outdoor access leading directly to the dune path and the beach. An exterior staircase curtained by a wooden screen leads to both the second floor and the roof deck. The main living space is located on the second floor to capture the ocean view. The space contains cooking, eating, and living functions all in one room. Stackable sliding doors open the space up completely to the deck that is created by the volume below. The fireplace captures two of these sliding panels, turning the room into one large outdoor porch.

SHORE HOUSE
AMAGANSETT, NY, USA

Architect: Stelle Lomont Rouhani Architects
Interior designer: Yabu Pushelberg
Landscape architect: LaGuardia Design
Year of completion: 2012
No. of rooms: 6
Gross floor area/site area: 265 m²/3,715 m²
Luxury features: hot tub

The master bedroom and the master bathroom are located on the second floor, adequately screened from the road by the wooden slats and vegetation. On the roof, a spa and outdoor shower overlook the ocean. The side of the house facing the beach is open and at night the lights shine out, casting a warm and welcoming glow across the dunes. Inside, simple furnishings reflect the purpose of the space; this is a house where one should spend time outdoors, enjoying the sun, sand and sea whenever possible.

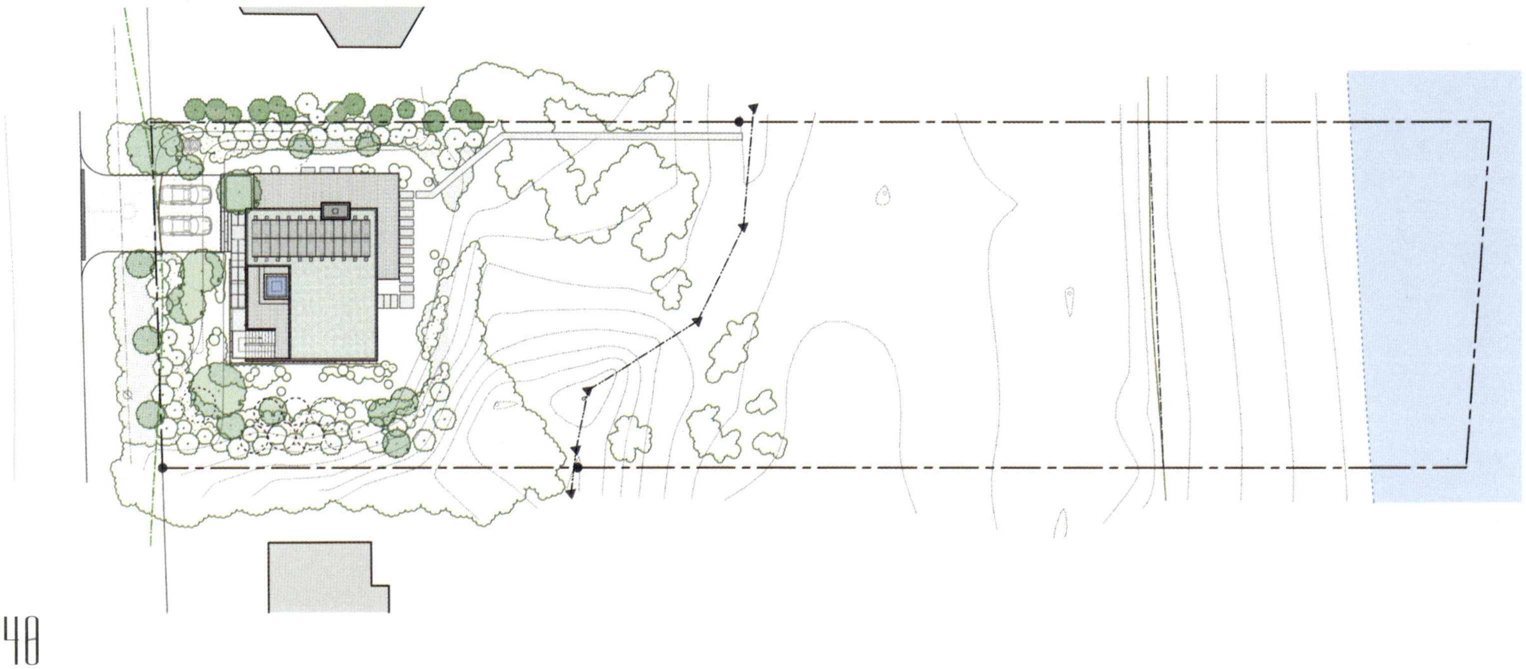

A small piece of heaven nestled in amongst the dunes. Outdoors is the place to be!

HOUSE ON THE ISLAND OF KRK
ISLAND OF KRK, CROATIA

The client's wish was to build a vacation home with a prospect of becoming a permanent home at a later date. The house is located on the island of Krk on the Adriatic coast and is separated from the beach by a green zone and a promenade. All the important facilities are oriented towards the sea view, and the space is organized to be used comfortably by three families at the same time.

The bedrooms are located on the lower floors with direct access to the pool area, while the living area is housed on the top floor, making the most of the stunning views. The outside spaces vary in character, from a completely open terrace to semi-open and completely covered. A large terrace and swimming pool are oriented towards the ocean so that residents can enjoy the views while relaxing in the pool. The large windows and openings on both sides of the house allow for a pleasant draft, providing passive cooling and some relief from the hot summer weather.

Architect: DVA Arhitekta
Year of completion: 2012
No. of rooms: 4 bedrooms
Gross floor area/site area: 386 m²/800 m²
Luxury features: swimming pool

The design of the house takes some aspects of traditional architecture, for example the white and gray volume, natural stone combined with smooth white plaster and a flat roof; but it is characterized by its modern elegance and a striking simplicity of form. The natural stone base shares a dialogue with the rocky coastline, so that when one looks up at the house from the shoreline it appears almost as an extension of its surroundings. The stone walls that are prevalent everywhere on this sloping terrain also help to integrate the large volume on its stone base into the surrounding environment.

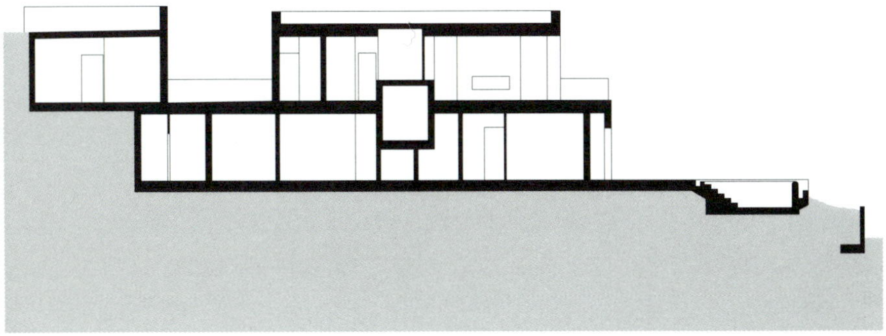

Natural stone and the use of wood connect this modern vacation home to the rough coastal environment.

MONA VALE HOUSE
MONA VALE, AUSTRALIA

The client of this project has a long-standing interest in building sustainability, developed through working at the Sustainable Energy Development Authority (SEDA). With this interest in mind, he approached CHROFI to design a house that would demonstrate a number of active and passive sustainable initiatives whilst accommodating a contemporary coastal lifestyle. The project is sited on the south side of Mona Vale Headland and offers extensive views over Mona Vale Beach to the south. This south-facing aspect and the narrow site proportions combine to limit the passive design potential and accordingly establish the key design challenge for the project.

The architects' response orients the house towards the view to the south, but opens up the roof at the center of the house with a large north-facing skylight to admit winter sun to the south-facing living areas and to trap and hold the warmth of the winter sun using the thermal mass of the structure. Other sustainability measures include a 15,000-liter rainwater storage tank combined with gray water recycling to minimize water usage, the use of evacuated tubes for in-floor heating as well as hot water supply and photovoltaic solar panels to provide electricity back to the grid.

Architect: CHROFI
Interior designer: CHROFI
Collaborators: Simpson Design & Associates, Northrop, ExParrot, Cave & Associates
Year of completion: 2005
No. of rooms: 3 bedrooms
Gross floor area/site area: 265 m²/1,124 m²

The house can be 'zoned' to three separate areas; the sunroom at the back, the bedrooms and hallway, and the living area in the front. This assists in the retention of heat during the winter months. Cross ventilation is carefully considered within the whole house. The front living area ventilates through a series of louvers in a bank of high level clerestory. The bedrooms also have cross ventilation via fanlight windows above the doors.

Architectural experiments: The house is a 'test-bed' for sustainable features.

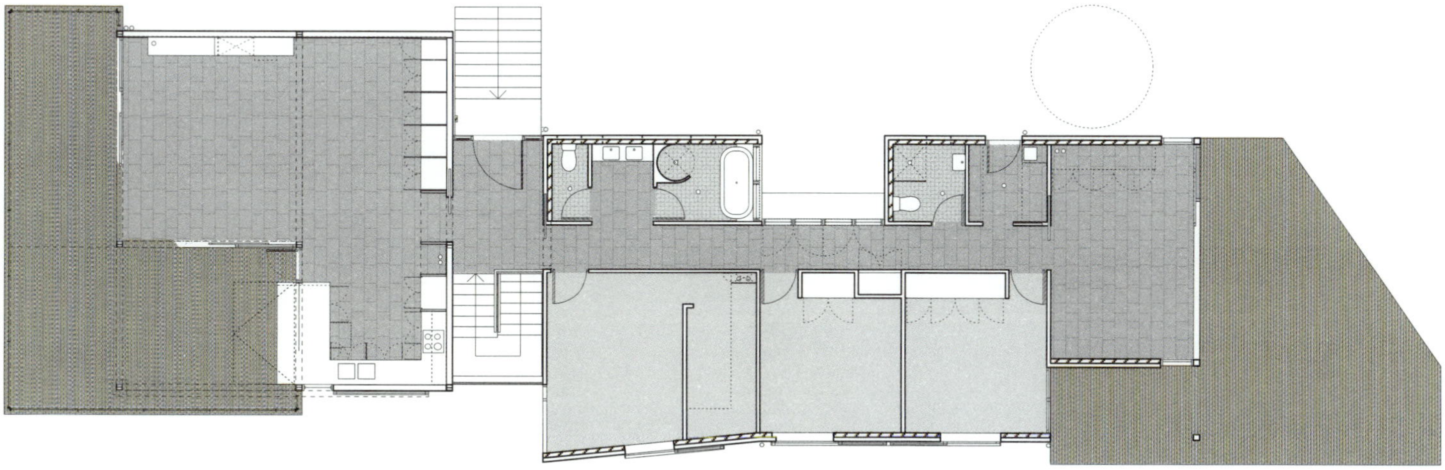

This house is situated in a coastal area and occupies a steeply sloping plot with nice views. It is situated at the top of the site, next to the entrance. The compact volume is pierced by four openings: The terrace, drying area, playground and garden. The patios provide optimal cross ventilation as well as exposure to the sun and draw a wealth of natural light into the house. In summer the living room can be opened out and is almost like a large covered terrace, exposed to the gentle sea breeze. During the winter months, a large balcony on the entrance level offers wide-sweeping views over the harbor. The construction is simple yet elegant, with ceramic load-bearing walls, steel pillars and concrete slab floors. Traditional local materials have also been used, such as the bamboo on the porch. These help to give the design an individual character. The large openings cut into the volume, combined with the use of bamboo help to give the house a more dynamic and lightweight appearance. This is also enhanced by the slim pillars, which support the upper level but disrupt the views as little as possible.

HOUSE WITH FOUR PATIOS
CALA D'OR, MALLORCA, SPAIN

Architect: Flexo Arquitectura
Year of completion: 2010
No. of rooms: 4
Gross floor area/site area: 275 m²/1,000 m²
Luxury features: swimming pool

The patio area reaches out towards the wooden decking and the swimming pool, incorporating the pool into the design and giving the entire volume the sense of being a unified whole. The side of the house where the entrance is located is more solid in appearance, offering privacy from the interested gaze of passersby.

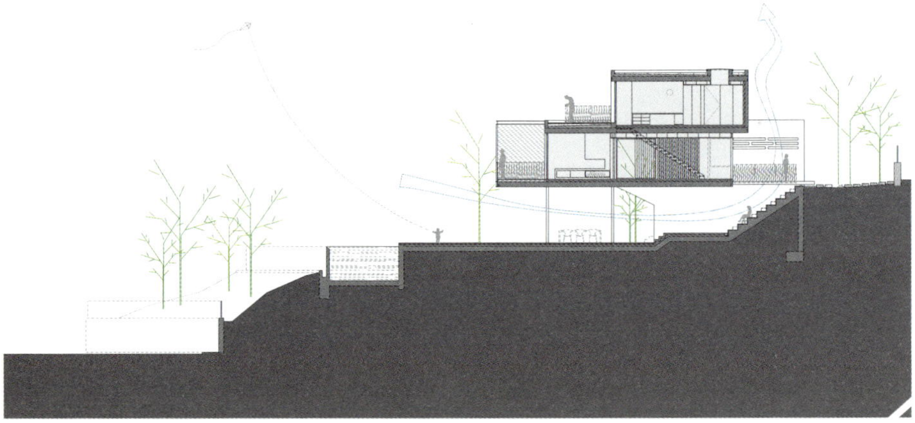

Bamboo has the outstanding ability to absorb large amounts of CO_2.

SCAPEHOUSE
CAPE LIPTRAP, AUSTRALIA

This coastal residence is located on a stunning isolated site in eastern Victoria on former farmland. The design is an investigation of how an idealised conception of "house" is transformed by its context and use. The site has extraordinary qualities: the harsh prevailing winds of the Roaring Forties; sloping site; and sublime panoramic views from Cape Liptrap to Wilson's Promontory. The residence requires maximum flexibility as a beach home that could accommodate varying sleeping needs — anything from a single guest to burgeoning family summer holidays.

As a point of departure, the sectional character of the design adopts an idealised child-like profile of a gabled house. However, this reading of the architecture is subverted by a reorientation of the plan. The house twists to accommodate framed views and take advantage of the natural fall of the site, with two wings capturing significant views of the landscape to the east and west. These arms of the building create a sheltered area to the north side which provides a protected area from the prevailing winds. Inside, the wings are mediated by an ambiguous central space that operates as provisional gallery, entry, veranda, storage, dining, lounge and circulation zone. This contested area engages more directly with the landscape and environment and accommodates shifting patterns of use.

Architect: Andrew Simpson Architects
Year of completion: 2010
No. of rooms: 6
Gross floor area/site area: 113 m²/600 m²
Luxury features: private beach

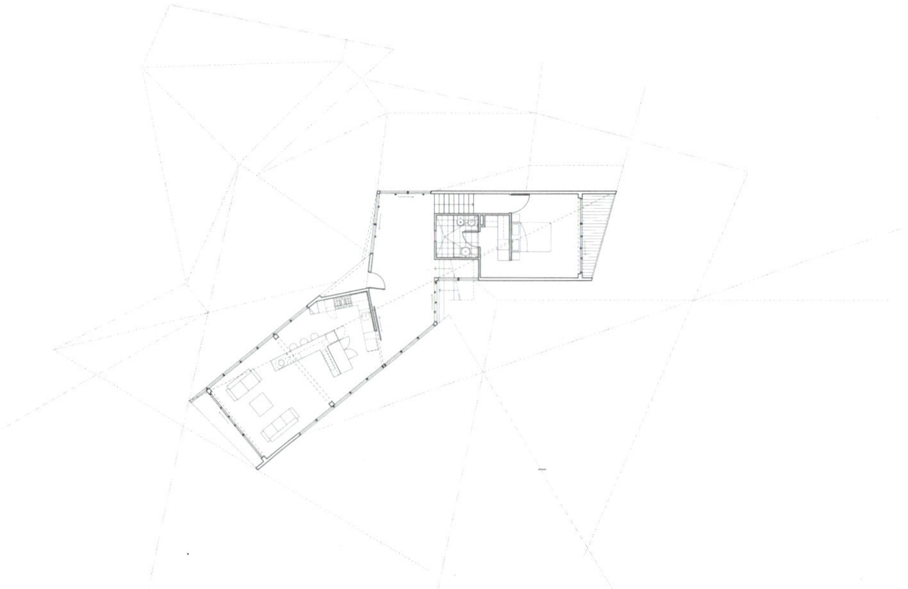

Like many beach houses located on Australia's southern coastline, this project faced the dilemma of a site with spectacular views, but oriented to the south. The design response was to articulate openings to reveal (and conceal) specific vistas, inviting the inhabitants of the house to speculate both on the nature of 'viewing' and also their relationship with the landscape and its mediation through architecture.

Abstract geometry blurs one's perception of the building's scale and depth; it becomes an oscillating silhouette.

FIDAR BEACH HOUSE
JBEIL, LEBANON

This summer beach house for a family of five and three guests is situated in Jbeil, along the northern coast of Lebanon. Despite its rugged nature, the site is restricted by a mandatory 10-meter shoreline setback. This limits the project's placement to a relatively flat area between a secondary private road and the sea. The project aims at preserving the natural qualities of the site by seamlessly integrating itself to the existing landscape.

The overall design strategy had major implications on the programmatic and tectonic concept of the beach house. Public spaces are placed at site entry level and private spaces are positioned at the lower levels. The top level is constructed as a platform raised on short columns, with the intention of minimal alteration of the natural rocky landscape, while enhancing the view of the shoreline. The edge of the deck is lowered, along with the strip adjacent to it in order to remove any obstructions in front of the view. The elevation and lowering of the terraces creates a sequence of seating conditions that further animates the outdoor deck.

Architect: Raëd Abillama Architects
Interior designer: Raëd Abillama Architects
Year of completion: 2011
No. of rooms: 11
Gross floor area/site area: 506 m^2/3,100 m^2
Luxury features: swimming pool

The stairwell and entrance hall are grouped with lighting and ventilation shafts to create a threshold between levels of public spaces. The outdoor pergola and shower cabin further extend this demarcation line. The platform rests on the bedrooms which are placed as close as possible to the shore. The swimming pool offers stunning views of the ocean and of nearby hills, joining directly onto the terrace at the top of the house.

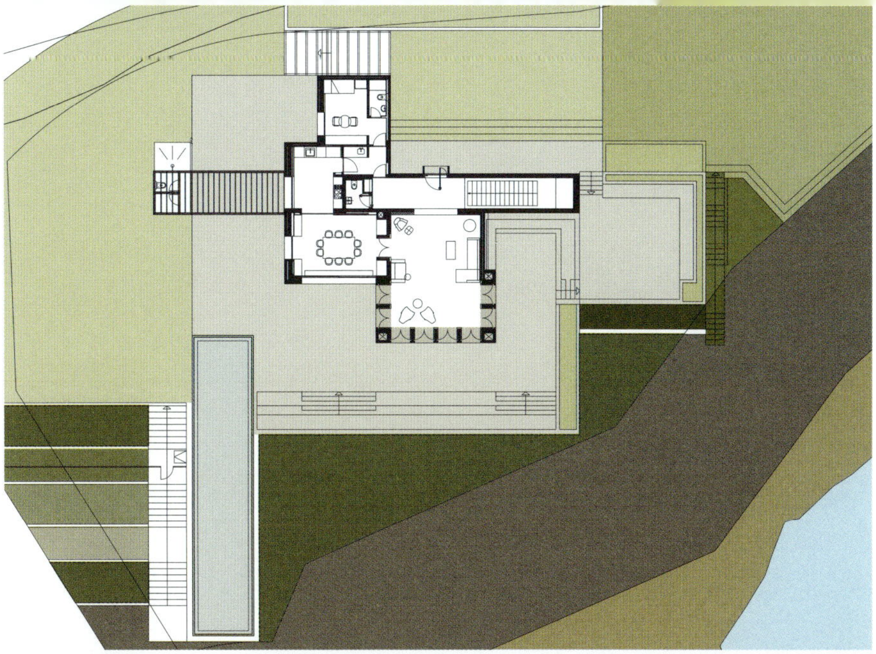

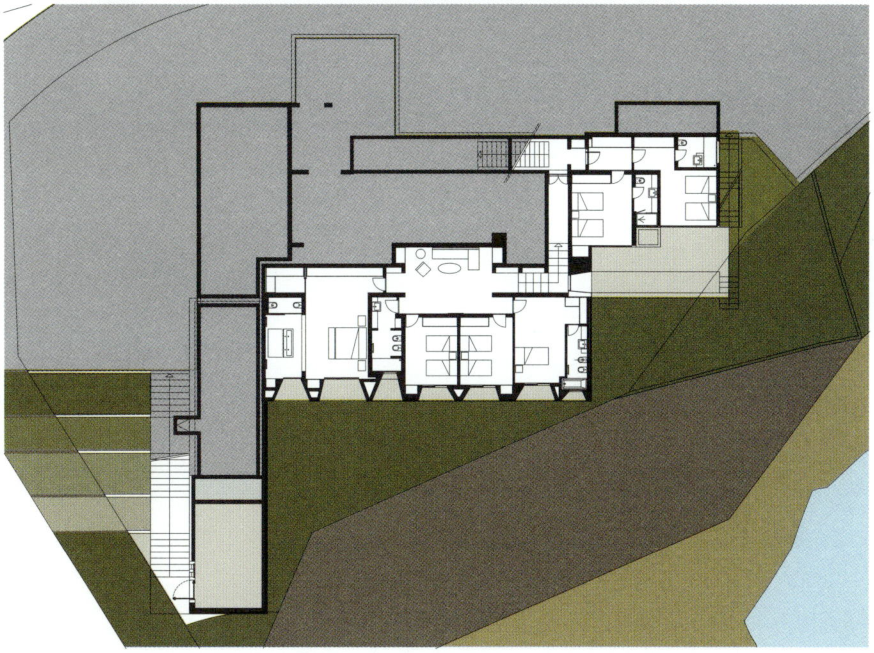

Choose between relaxing in the sun on the terrace, swimming in the pool or taking a stroll along the rugged coast line.

CASA Q
PLAYA MISTERIO, PERU

Infinite rolling dunes, reaching from the desert to the rocky cliffs and facing the Pacific Ocean, create a unique natural environment. Casa Q is located at Beach Club Misterio, located 117 kilometers south of Lima, Peru. Challenging the stillness of the surroundings, Casa Q is the materialization of a young couple's dream, a 'floating volume' that offers more than enough space for a family in the future. The volume is supported by circular columns placed by intuition, as a dance, instead of forcibly in a grid. The dancing columns are accompanied by sliding glass panels that define the communal areas; the living and dining space and terrace can either be combined or separated by opening or closing the glass panels to create a large space for social occasions to protect the house from the weather.

The rest of the house – guest rooms, kitchen and services – are tastefully secluded at the back of the sloped site. Every room in the house enjoys views of the horizon. The living area opens out onto the large pool, encased in a blue basin, which almost makes it appear as if it is a solid block of water, somehow defying the pull of gravity.

Architect: Longhi Architects
Year of completion: 2010
No. of rooms: 6
Gross floor area/site area: 500 m^2/420 m^2
Luxury features: swimming pool, private bar

The entire front of the house is glazed, giving it an open and welcoming appearance. The design has been very carefully considered with all seating elements and living areas oriented to enjoy the views, and the more private areas located towards the back of the house. The columns have also been carefully placed to interrupt views of the ocean as little as possible.

House overboard! From below the large volume appears to almost float above the pool.

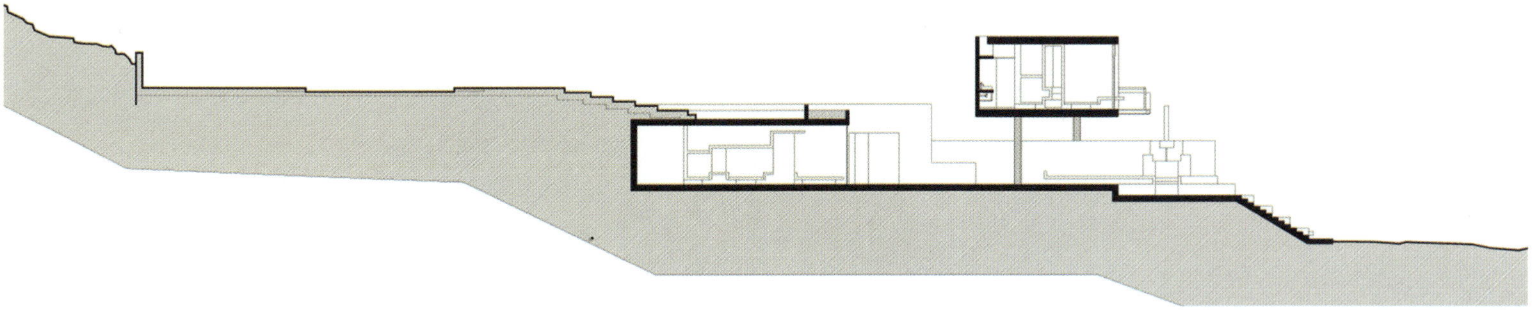

MAVA HOUSE
CACHAGUA, CHILE

Architect: Gubbins Architects
Year of completion: 2011
No. of rooms: 4
Gross floor area/site area: 360 m²/2,250 m²
Luxury features: swimming pool

The focus point of this design was the creation of a large terrace that would provide space for relaxing outdoor leisure time with views of the nearby ocean. The large horizontal terrace reinforces the relationship between those using it and the distant horizon, communicating a feeling of never-ending space. This stretching horizontal orientation contrasts the stark verticality of the nearby cliffs. The program is divided into two units; this provides the architectural support for the terrace. To the south is a large metal and wood "beam-wall" which protects the house against the south-west winds and shelters the entrance from the sun. The architecture of the two longitudinal volumes breaks up the space and folds it into a series of slabs and beams that allows for big distances between supports without spoiling the ocean view.

The narrow pool is situated right at the edge of the terrace. This makes the most of the views and when persons feel the need to take a break from swimming, they can simply lean on the side and enjoy views stretching out towards the horizon – it is of course also the perfect spot from where to watch the sunrise or sunset.

The volume is cut into the sloping site, so that the height has a minimal impact on the esthetics of the site. The volume is also plain, which helps to emphasize the surrounding nature in all its glory. It is broken up into a series of different connected volumes and levels, making it appear less solid and dominating and therefore more dynamic.

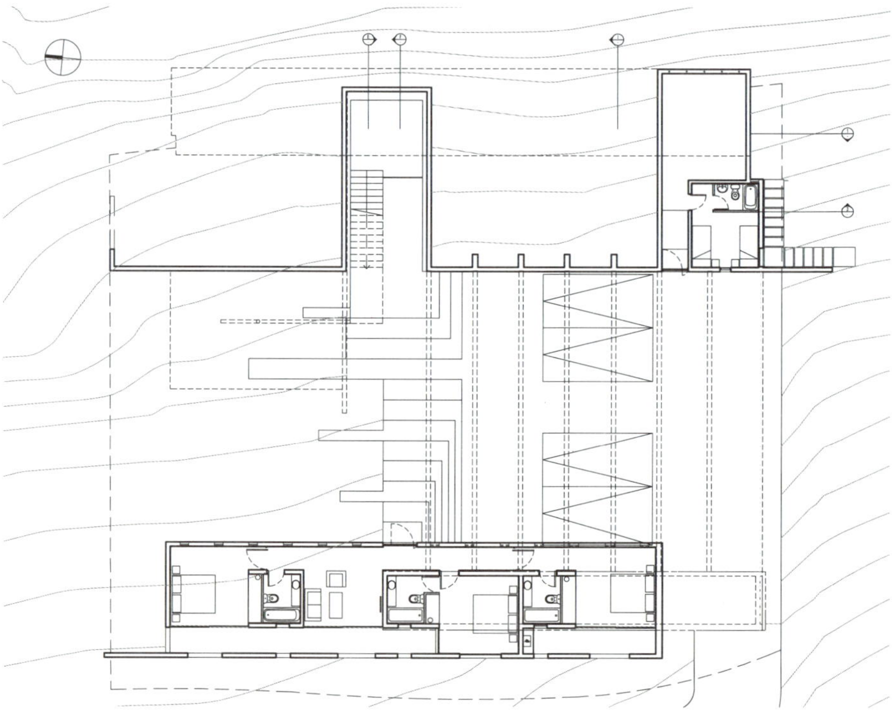

As the country, so the design: spacious, infinite and sublime.

This project is a flexible contemporary family residence, built on a spectacular but challenging site, which is positioned on the ridge below Lions Head with 270-degree views of the Atlantic Ocean, Camps Bay and the Twelve Apostles beyond. It is an extreme corner site – a compact wedge of steep, predominately south-facing hillside with exposure to prevailing winds and its longest boundary along a busy road. A key strategy to create a generous level for principal living rooms was to elevate the main level on a plinth comprising guest bedrooms and secondary spaces such as the gym, study and garage. The ground floor is partially set into the steep site, thereby maximizing the living level and raising it above the noisy provincial road. The first and second floors were then set back, fragmented and rotated to create a central but sheltered external terrace. A glass bridge forms the link between the fragmented upper levels and permits north sunlight to shine between the bedroom wings and into the central areas on the south side of the house.

CLIFTON 2A
CAPE TOWN, SOUTH AFRICA

Architect: SAOTA
Interior designer: Janine Lazard
Year of completion: 2014
Site area: 1,120 m²
Luxury features: swimming pool, gym, massage room, outside shower

Visitors are welcomed by a sculpture set into a water feature and, through full height glazing, by glimpses of the mountains beyond. Monolithic stairs are suspended above and filter shafts of refracted morning light, creating a sense of calm. A blue mosaic rim flow pool runs parallel to the terrace and brings sea and sky into the living spaces. The family bedrooms are strategically positioned on the second floor with extensive views and opulent interiors.

Wide windows serve to frame the stunning views of the Atlantic Ocean.

This house is located in Tunquén, in the midst of a striking landscape just 45 minutes from Santiago. Mirador is perched on a clifftop, which provides residents with a bird's-eye view of the surroundings. Because of its location and architecture, the house is visible from afar. It rises from the ground and those entering ascend to the main floor by means of a ramp. The interior comprises a large meeting space connected to two terraces that open to the sea and the countryside respectively on opposite sides. The center of the main space is a double-height area through which sunlight enters during the morning and the evening. The roof terrace can also be accessed from here, via a spiral staircase. The position of the house makes it the perfect location for enjoying the sunrise or sunset, offering uninterrupted views of the horizon. The basic rectangular shape of the volume is interrupted by incisions on both sides; deep openings have been cut into the volume to provide space for a terrace slightly raised above the ground.

CASA MIRADOR
TUNQUÉN, CHILE

Architect: Gubbins Architects
Year of completion: 2015
No. of rooms: 2 bedrooms
Gross floor area/site area: 135 m²/5,009 m²

The fact that the house is raised above the site gives it an almost modern lighthouse quality, enhanced by large windows that allow the light to shine out like a beacon at night. The lighthouse reference is also continued inside the house, with a spiraling staircase leading to the upper levels. The sandy-color of the concrete harmonizes with the surroundings, giving the volume a more natural appearance.

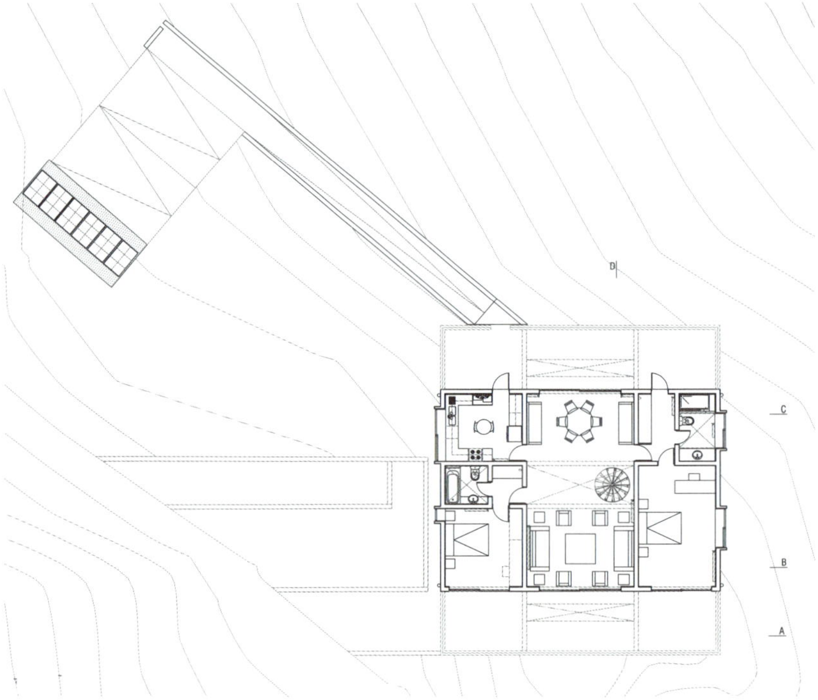

Feeling like on the top of the world in the midst of rough cliffs and the vast sea.

SLAUGHTERHOUSE BEACH HOUSE
MAUI, HAWAII, USA

Located on a sheer rock bluff above a well-known surfing spot, this house was designed as a family retreat. Drawing on the concept of a surf hut, three connected huts – the main sleeping areas, living quarters, and guest suites – follow the topography in a gentle curve. The 73,000-square meter site had been neglected and taken over by invasive plant species; an important goal for the project was to heal the site by returning the majority of the landscape to native plants.

The huts' corrugated metal roofs take their inspiration from traditional Hawaiian roofs – as popularized by the architect C. W. Dickey. Studies of the site revealed virtually constant winds. Using the Dickey-style roof as a starting point, the design was turbocharged, deliberately shaping roof forms and openings to allow breezes to pull hot air out. The boldness of the roof forms is matched by large operable window walls that are a continuation of Kundig's previous explorations at projects such as Chicken Point Cabin in northern Idaho. The central hut's window walls swing up on two sides, allowing the hut to open fully to the landscaped hillside, to the pool and to the ocean.

Architect: Olson Kundig
Project team: Tom Kundig, Kirsten R. Murray, Steven Rainville
Year of completion: 2009
No. of rooms: 7
Gross floor area/site area: 418 m²/73,000 m²
Luxury features: swimming pool

The kitchen island defies expectations by extending through this window wall when closed. The large Ipe wood decks and screened walkways connecting the huts almost double the home's livable area. The materials are low maintenance and virtually fire-proof: steel, wood, and rammed earth walls that are a mixture of local soil and concrete. The resulting structure blends in with its surroundings.

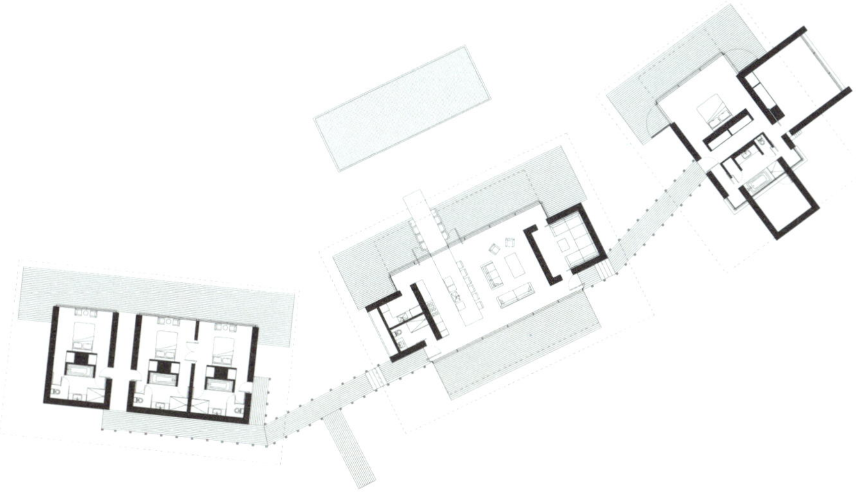

Huge window walls offer panoramic views of the ocean.

This design focuses on the importance of establishing a connection between light and the horizon. The shining sun and the blue of the sea serve as the starting points that guide the architectural plan. The vernacular elements of the design are embedded in western, modern principles, but it is also inspired by Roman traditions and nowadays Israeli architecture. Alongside the functional, modern character of this design, one also feels the sheer mass, the asymmetry, and a sense of dismantled space. The outer, linear envelope of the building evokes the International Style, while subverting it to its own purpose; protecting the building from overheating under the desert sun. Not only do the windows offer a resplendent view, they also provide comfort. The house uses certain traditional architectural traits, such as the use of a flat roof and a predominantly white volume – this is typical of architecture in a hot climate.

A HOUSE BY THE SEA
SHAVEY ZION, ISRAEL

Architect: Pitsou Kedem Architects
Initial design and planning: Irene Goldberg, Pitsou Kedem
Architect in charge: Tamar Berger
Lighting designer: Orly Avron Alkabes
Year of completion: 2015
Gross floor area/site area: 280 m²/700 m²
Luxury features: swimming pool

The stripes cut into the façade continue inside, where white walls, galleries and doors all feature the same stripes. This gives a sense of fluidity and continuation, where inside and outside are not opposed, but rather come together to form a coherent whole. The huge floor-to-ceiling windows are really magnificent. Sliding glass doors on the lower floor can also be opened out, making the terrace part of the living area and blurring the boundary between inside and outside.

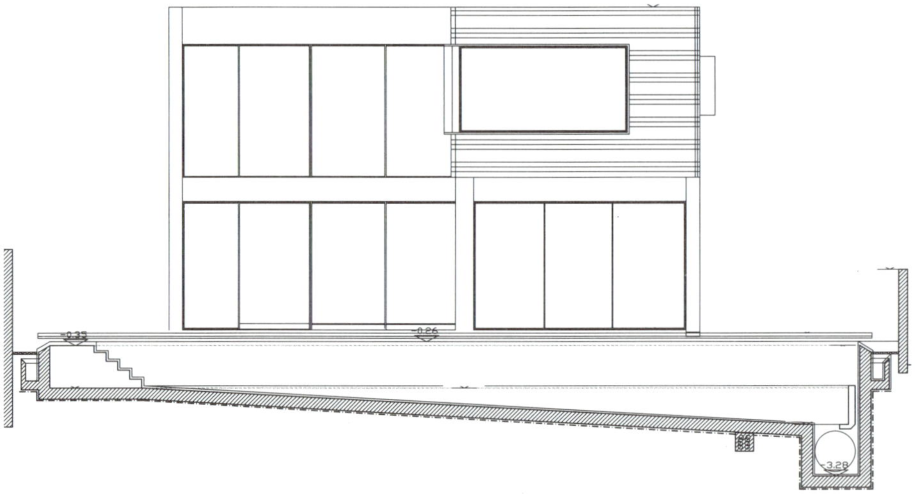

Shavey Zion means: “Returnees to Zion”. The immediate proximity to the Mediterranean Sea could tempt one to stay there forever.

OVD 919
CAPE TOWN, SOUTH AFRICA

The brief was to create a spectacular home that makes the most of the stunning 360-degree views of the mountains and the ocean. The site enjoys an excellent position on the mountain ridge below Lions Head with views of Robben Island to the north and Camps Bay and the Twelve Apostles to the south. Working with a relatively steep site and the fact that the southern boundary is shared with a national park, the design had to take a very sensitive approach. The secondary spaces were carefully positioned on the lower levels to limit excavation. From the road, these levels are concealed by a large north-facing landscape wall – its customized angular design achieves a natural result.

The main living areas, pool terrace and garden are located on the lower levels with the family bedrooms strategically positioned on the uppermost level for privacy. The 'layering' of the house permits different experiences in different spaces. From the main stairs the linearity of the customized cast bronze coffee bar leads one into the kitchen. The kitchen in turn spills into the dining room and the summer lounge with its high ceiling of ribbed concrete. The large gallery type spaces emphasize the magnetism of the site and its ever present backdrop of the mountains and the sea. A courtyard cuts into main living areas – its water feature and delicate weathered Cor-Ten screen ensure a tranquil and sheltered space.

Architect: SAOTA
Interior designer: Debra Parkington
Year of completion: 2014
Gross floor area/site area: 979 m²/2,879 m²
Luxury features: swimming pool

The thin eaves of the zinc roof are also delicate in contrast to the massive beams below and appear to hover above the upper level. The polished concrete floors of both the internal and external living areas ensure their seamless continuity. The timelessness of natural oak is celebrated and combined with feature brass insets for bedroom floors and all internal joinery.

This house's variety of spaces gives the impression of going on safari within your own four walls.

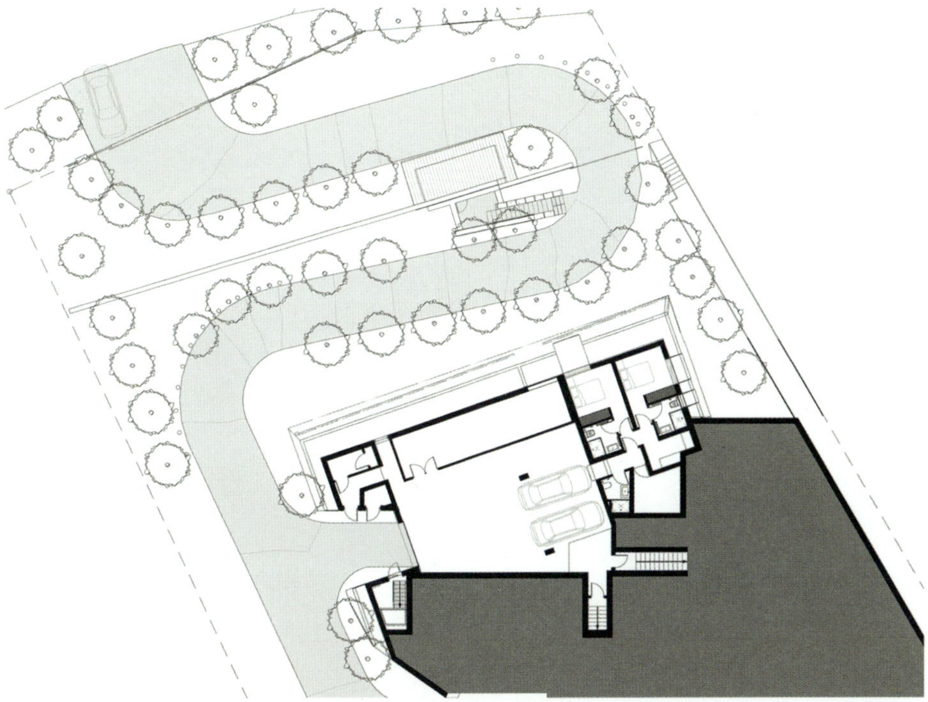

The philosophy of Mandalay Beach Villas is crisp, clear and simple. Against a backdrop of unerring modern style and sophistication, the architects have created an unforgettable contemporary tropical experience. Beyond the design-led, classy environs, an impressive balance between form and function, inside and out, modern and tropical has been created. Mandalay Beach Villas is a collection of beachfront pool villas in contemporary modern design. The secure and gated luxury estate offers the ultimate in island accommodation, matching exclusivity with privacy. Facing the white sandy expanse of Laem Noi Beach, right next to Four Seasons Resort Samui and backed by lush palm stands, each of the exclusive villas has its own private courtyard, giving approximately 350–550 square meters of living space, with 17–35 meters of beach frontage each. The height of the villas has been kept to the minimum in order to avoid disrupting the view, so a number of different volumes have been built in order to avoid building upwards.

MANDALAY BEACH VILLAS
KOH SAMUI, THAILAND

Architect: PJC Wood
Interior designer: Mandalay Samui Developments
Year of completion: 2014
Gross floor area/site area: 350 m²/800 m²
Luxury features: swimming pool, intelligent LED lighting system, turn-key designer furniture package, digital entertainment system

Inside, the emphasis of the interior design is on elegance, with wood combined with smooth white walls, limited ornamentation and large windows. The number of furnishings has been kept to the minimum, which emphasizes the sense of space. All of the villas are oriented towards the beach, making the most of the sweeping ocean views and minimizing the distance to the beach.

Inhale and exhale – an oasis of calm for relaxation right next to the beach.

Rock house replaces an older building that was located on the site. In order to obtain the relevant planning permits, the project had to be well-adjusted to suit the terrain, both in terms of shape, scale, material and color. The house and terraces have been partially built using existing stone walls, the parts of the walls that are new have been built using stones from blasting at the site. A number of incisions have been cut into the low elongated volume to create outdoor areas shielded from the wind, while embraced and protected by the house itself. These incisions also help to reduce the sheer scale of the building and, together with the local variations of the section, they also help the building to establish a dialogue with the form of the nearby cliffs. On the outer perimeter of the terraces and the pool, a glass fence has also been erected to offer protection from the wind. Glass was chosen because it offers adequate protection, but doesn't obstruct views of the sea.

ROCK HOUSE
VESTFOLD, NORWAY

Architect: Jarmund/Vigsnæs Arkitekter
Year of completion: 2009
No. of rooms: 6
Gross floor area: 300 m²
Luxury features: swimming pool

The design is noteable for its careful consideration of the environment. The house emphasizes rather than detracts from the raw beauty of the site. The materials used respond to the surroundings and the house simply looks as if it belongs there, perched on a rocky outcrop and calmly looking out to the sea; as if it has always been there and always will be there.

Beautiful, weatherproof and a sustainable alternative to tropical hardwood: Norwegian Kebony wood wraps the house.

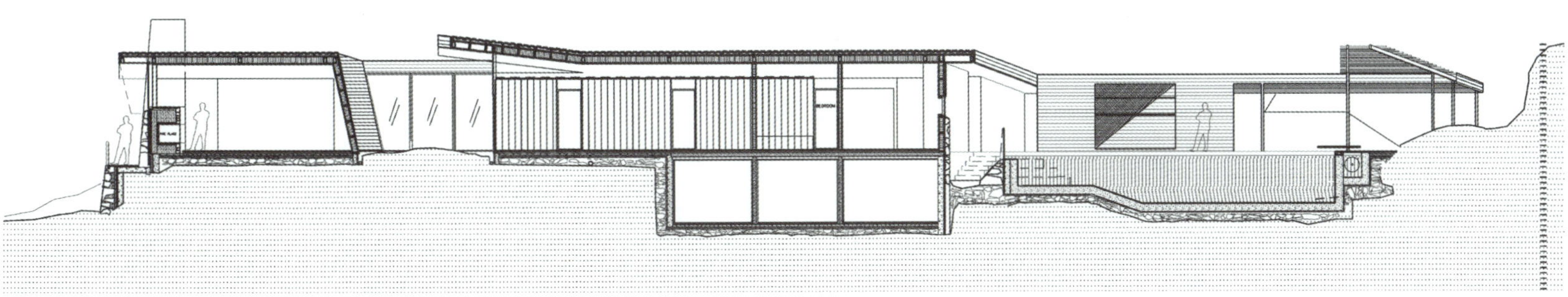

Azuris, located on Hamilton Island, is a three-bedroom holiday home cascading down a hillside overlooking the Coral Sea. The design responds to three key elements of its island location: light, air and water. The simplicity of Azuris is a tribute to the beauty of its location. The home comprises a series of simple spaces carved out of robust masonry, generating a sense of both weight and lightness, and ensuring longevity and low maintenance in the sub-tropical climate. On approach, the house is visible as a green roof planted with native species, drawing the eye out further to the ocean's horizon beyond. An expansive pool is wrapped around the main pavilion, creating a dramatic design element, vital to introduce water's cooling and visual delight to the interior. The surface of the luxurious pool transfers seamlessly into the horizon with its unique ocean panorama, with other islands and Australia's mainland to the west. The house spans between two dominant painted anthracite-gray side walls for privacy; with the living area, main bedroom and swimming pool at the top, and the guest rooms and an undercover sheltered terrace on the lower story.

AZURIS
HAMILTON ISLAND, AUSTRALIA

Architect: Renato D'Ettorre Architects
Year of completion: 2011
No. of rooms: 9
Gross floor area/site area: 222 m²/2,336 m²
Luxury features: outdoor terrace pool, private beach, tropical gardens

The western façade opens up entirely to the view of the ocean, whereas the two side walls and a natural stone wall anchor the building into the slope. The two gray privacy walls and exposed concrete elements blend in with the volcanic rock of the island and the native eucalyptus trees. The courtyard is a quiet contemplative place with a cooling reflection pond with waterlillies. On the lower level directly under the swimming pool are two guest bedrooms with framed views set within deep terraces providing shade from the hot westerly sun. Also a generously proportioned open under-cover living area is shaded throughout the day, ideal for escaping the heat whilst being closer to the natural vegetation and ideal for sunset viewing.

An architectural promenade between the land and the sea.

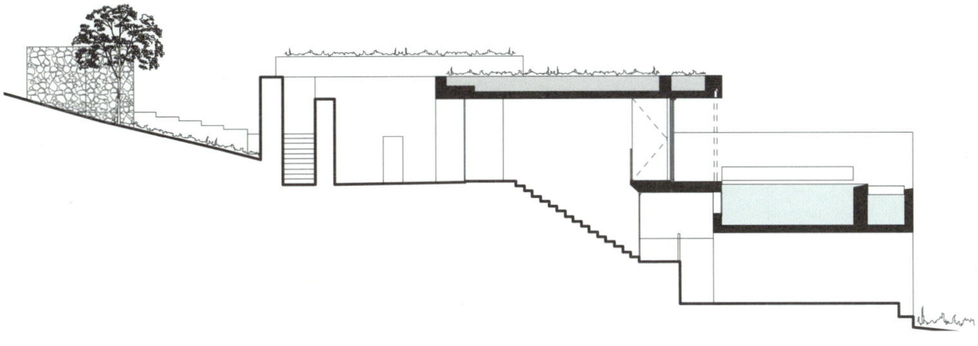

The owners purchased an existing beach cottage in Kirkland, Washington in 2008. The architects planned to remove the old cottage but upcycled the recently upgraded foundation by building a new three-story home on it. The site is stunning. This house sits less than 12 meters from the water and squares off with Mount Rainier and the length of the lake. The architects were committed to reusing the existing foundation and thus weren't automatically poised to take advantage of passive heating and cooling, views and well placed outdoor spaces. The architects considered the awkwardly shaped footprint of the foundation and then began to disintegrate the footprint by projecting the upper two stories beyond and subtracting from that footprint, setting up a series of overhangs, protected outdoor spaces, framed views and cross ventilation. Exterior materials were important to consider since the house was going to have to endure extreme weather. A metal siding was selected, with a kynar finish and Hardiepanel.

KIRKLAND RESIDENCE
KIRKLAND, WA, USA

Architect: Allied8
Structural engineer: Swenson Say Faget
Year of completion: 2012
No. of rooms: 13
Gross floor area/site area: 325 m²/397 m²
Luxury features: sauna, private jetty, boat launch

On the street side, which is well protected from the weather, predominately cedar siding was used to give warmth to the entry experience and to the neighborhood streetscape as a whole. A steel moment frame was used to open up the side of the house to the fabulous view. The entire glass front between the living area and the terrace can be opened up, giving the feeling of being on a boat. This design feature helps to incorporate the scenery into the design of the house itself, creating a situation where architecture and surroundings become one.

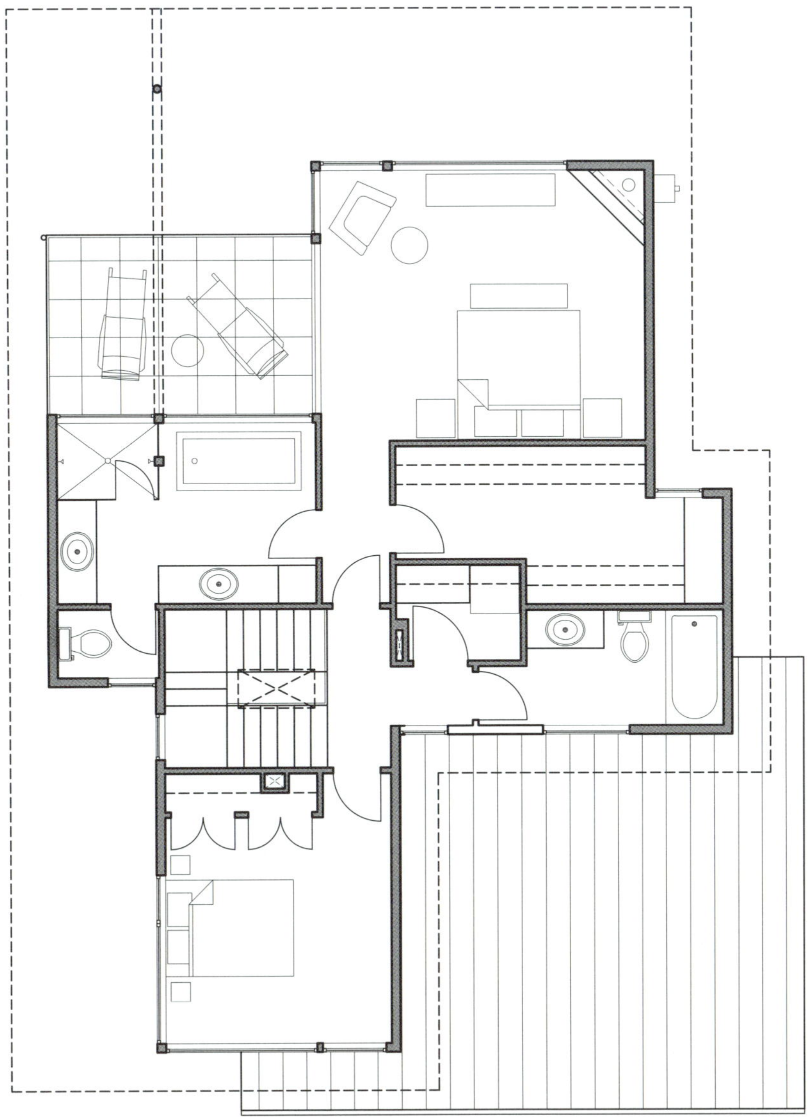

In this residence you feel more like you are in a boat than in a house.

Solis draws inspiration from its magnificent location and Mediterranean coastal architecture: simple, permeable volumes that open and unfold, capturing distant views of tropical waters and island life. Built over three interlocking levels the design intends to highlight the relationship between the interior and exterior environment and to capture the serenity of the natural surroundings of the built form. Emphasizing the importance of being connected with the island's sub-tropical environment was a key intent of the design. Materials and finishes were kept to a bare minimum so as not to create a sense of excess. The house is mostly seen from the elevated access road and neighboring properties. The small, articulated planted roofs offer an esthetically pleasing profile against the azure ocean and the hardy roof planting contributes to preserving the integrity of the surrounding natural beauty. Terraces are fluid extensions of internal spaces capturing cooling breezes and allowing cross ventilation. The bedroom terraces frame magnificent views of water and gardens, distant lands and the horizon.

SOLIS
HAMILTON ISLAND, AUSTRALIA

Architect: Renato D'Ettorre Architects
Year of completion: 2010
No. of rooms: 12
Gross floor area/site area: 373 m²/2,335 m²
Luxury features: indoor and outdoor swimming pools, tropical gardens, gymnasium, private beach

The architecture incorporates a number of passive climate controls, such as deep overhangs that shade the interior, massive concrete walls or green roofs. Combining architectural energy-saving design principles along with material selection removes the need for other finishing trades and materials, requiring very little on-going maintenance, staying resilient to the extreme weather conditions of the tropics and avoiding regular repair and replacement maximizing the building's life span.

A main attraction of Hamilton Island is the impressive and colorful coral reefs.

LINK HOUSE
SYDNEY, AUSTRALIA

Located in Sydney and with a challenging 30 degree fall to the east down to the water's edge, the house was built on the existing footprint to maximize the spectacular views of the bay. Divided into two separate pavilions, the buildings are joined at ground level by a glass link over a reflective koi pond and surrounded by an internal courtyard and garden. The design blurs the boundary between inside and out, whilst maintaining a strong distinction between privacy and openness. Glass is the key to refining the rawness of the concrete walls and floors throughout.

The pavilions are designed in the true sense of the word: surrounded by gardens, terraces and breezeways emphasizing the bay environment of sun, air and views. The interior courtyard is the pivotal element of the design. It enables natural light to be introduced to all the main living spaces of the house whilst providing privacy from the surrounding houses. A bespoke pizza oven and built-in teppanyaki BBQ serve this pivotal entertaining area. The link between the pavilions acts as a visual and functional connection to the living pavilion with kitchen, dining and sitting areas, completed with fireplace. The sleeping pavilion, spread over three floors, contains the bedrooms, bathrooms, children's room and media lounge. The use of concrete as the main material was for its extreme resilience, excellent thermal properties and its textural qualities along with its ready-made finish, largely eliminating the use of renders and paint, as well as giving the surface finishes an instant patina.

Architect: Renato D'Ettorre Architects
Year of completion: 2012
No. of rooms: 12
Gross floor area/site area: 371 m²/1,026 m²
Luxury features: outdoor pool, wine cellar, harbor access with private jetty, steam room, cool room, chefs kitchen

The design incorporates a number of passive climate control measures such as thermal mass in the concrete slabs and walls; a 10,000-liter rainwater tank; and a garden roof which further insulates the building below and reduces storm water run-off. Deep overhangs and retractable blinds reduce the summer heat gain, while the impact of cross ventilation is amplified by reducing the building depth by the central courtyard and using bodies of water adjacent living spaces as cooling elements.

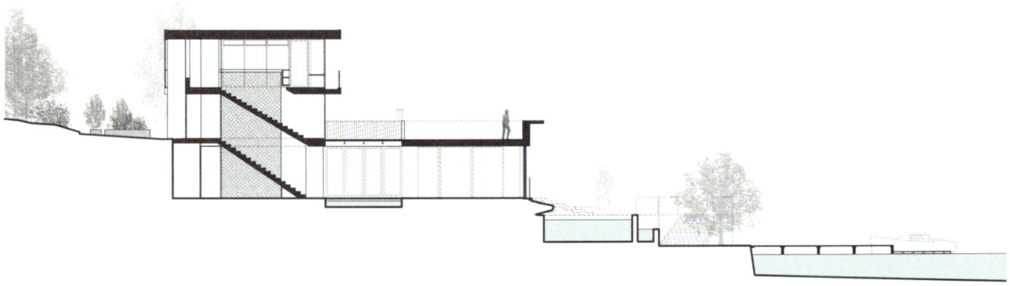

Cooling down from Sydney's summer heat has never been so easy.

Located on the coast in Paracas Bay, this design comprises a closed volume that extends along the total length of the plot. The main objective was to offer protection against the strong winds prevalent in this region. The volume expands, turns and embraces a wide open space, where all pathways are united around the swimming pool, terraces and landscape. The large windows along the length of the building draw a wealth of light inside, illuminating all of the rooms with a soft natural light. Protected by a huge exposed concrete mass, these spaces enjoy strong sunlight throughout the whole year. The building's esthetics are the direct result of the careful consideration of the environment where the building is located. Shapes, materials and colors seek to establish a dialogue with the textures and tones of the desert. The natural stone base and sandy-colored concrete harmonize with the sand of the beach and the low stone walls common in this area. The large windows not only make the most of the views, but also break up the solidity of the volume.

PARACAS HOUSE
PARACAS, PERU

Architect: Riofrio + Rodrigo Arquitectos, Roberto Riofrio Navarro, Micaela Rodrigo Graña
Year of completion: 2012
No. of rooms: 14
Gross floor area/site area: 680 m^2/1,322 m^2
Luxury features: swimming pool

The living room, dining room, kitchen, study and master bedroom are all located at the front of the house, making the most of the ocean view. Two guest bungalows with social areas and kitchenette are located adjacent to the main building. A small swimming pool is located next to the living room, so that anyone sitting in the living area can enjoy views of either the ocean or the pool.

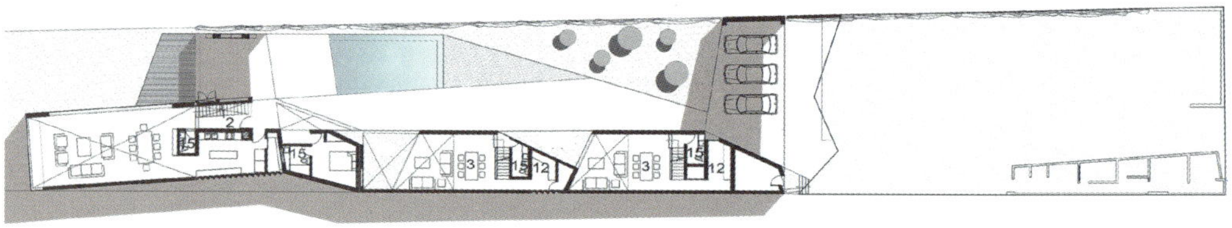

Paracas house combines modern esthetic with traditional building materials and a careful consideration of the site.

Located on 20,000 square meters of dense Ohia forest and just a stone's throw away from the beach, this cast-in-place concrete house frames indoor and outdoor living spaces along with views of the forest, the sky, and the coastline on Hawaii's Big Island. It continues the architect's exploration of a reductive architecture that enhances the experience of living in this compelling environment. The main feature of the house is a long concrete beam running the length of the building with only three short concrete walls supporting it along its massive span. Laminated beams and wooden planks make up the roof that hangs below it. The concrete beam allows for sizable spans of uninterrupted glass and covered outdoor space, which creates a permeable edge between man-made and nature. These huge open expanses amplify the sensation of living in the Ohia forest. The plan of the house is long and thin, with private and public areas divided by a lanai and bisected by a lap pool.

LAVAFLOW 7
PAHOA, HAWAII, USA

Architect: Craig Steely Architecture
Year of completion: 2013
No. of rooms: 12
Gross floor area/site area: 232 m^2/20,234 m^2
Luxury features: outdoor swimming pool

The narrow volume provides passive cooling through cross ventilation allowing for the elimination of mechanical air conditioning, consistent and diffused light quality in the rooms throughout the day, and a view of the forest, sky, and ocean from every room. Other sustainable features include a rainwater catchment system along with a solar heating system for domestic hot water.

Ohio trees are endemic to Hawaii and the first trees to grow on new lava flows.

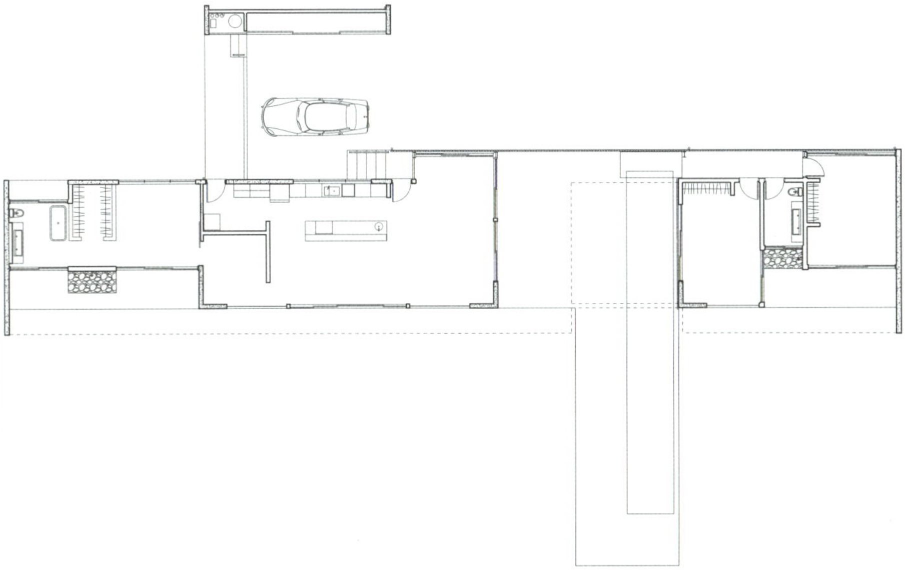

The requirement was for a large new family home maximizing the connection to the exterior spaces and views over Auckland harbor. To create a connection to the terraces, pool and gardens, the living areas were all placed one story below street level. The entrance is a sequence of descents into the home. The house was inspired by the harbor war bunkers in Auckland, dug into the cliff while open to the sea. In-situ and precast concrete was used to create a monastic simplicity, with textural contrast between structures rising from the ground against the walls located above.

The building is a built contradiction in terms, at once seemingly impenetrable and massive, and yet dissolving into the expansive horizon, opening out and embracing the views, drawing them almost inside the house and making the sweeping waterscape an integral part of the design. The large terrace really helps to form a connection between the house and the water, stretching out almost like a raft and giving the impression that it could float off at any moment.

HOBSON BAY HOUSE
AUCKLAND, NEW ZEALAND

Architect: Julian-Guthrie.com
Interior designer: Penny Hay
Year of completion: 2014
No. of rooms: 15
Gross floor area/site area: 740 m²/1,586 m²
Luxury features: swimming pool, spa, cabana, wine cellar, outdoor fireplace

The concrete was cast on timber, which provides grain and patina, giving it more character. Natural stone, raw brass, timber and steel provide material balance. The large expanses of glass help to dissolve the solid volume, breaking it up into smaller sections to provide a dynamic contrast of open and closed areas and thus giving the volume a more lightweight and less imposing appearance.

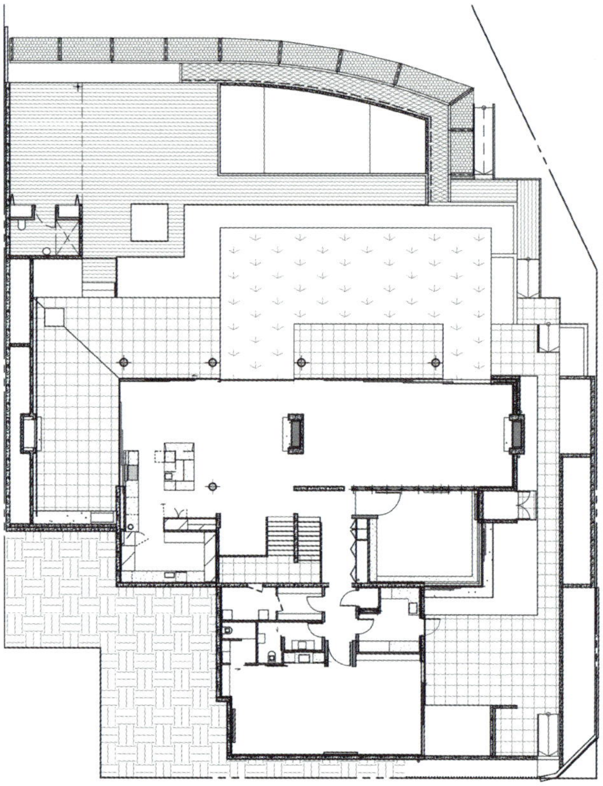

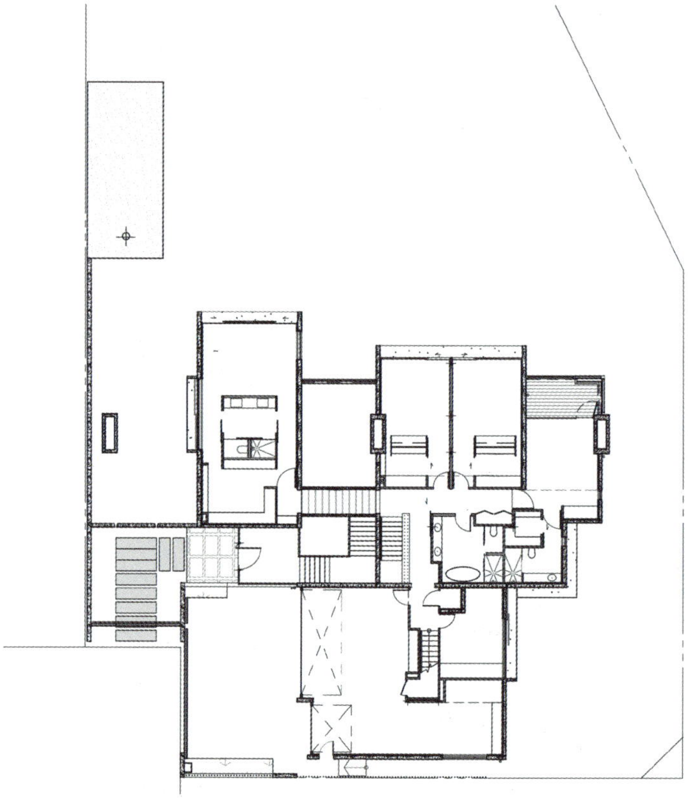

Inspired by harbor war bunkers in Auckland, this design creates a dynamic and surprisingly light volume.

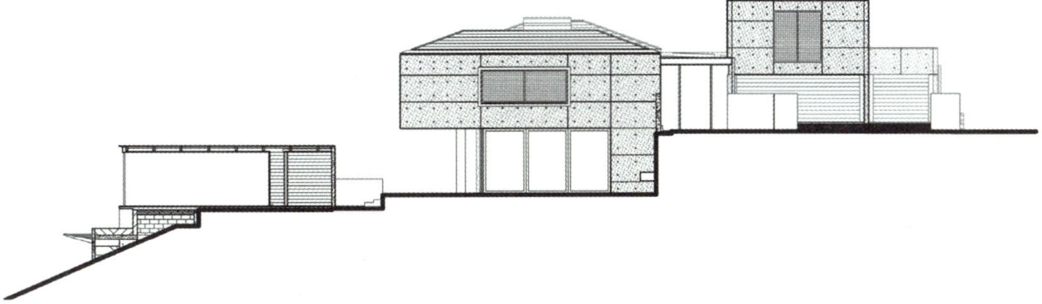

Located on a remote coastal site with vast ocean views the house is also very exposed to storms. The design concept is a low single-level home wrapped around a sheltered central courtyard space. This design is not only well-suited to the climate, making it less susceptible to strong winds and storms, but also causes minimal disruption to the site and the sweeping views. The building is a modern interpretation of a Maori pā, with a continuous series of timbered screens fortifying the house when in closed position, protecting the building when unoccupied. The slim pillars replace bearing walls and allow for an open-plan arrangement. This has the advantage of opening the house out to the views, so that regardless of where one is in the house there are as few barriers as possible between the inside and the surroundings. The courtyard functions as both an outdoor living space and a circulation space providing access to all parts of the house. This draws sunlight deep into all parts of the house from varying orientations throughout the day.

MAHIA HOUSE
MAHIA, NEW ZEALAND

Architect: Julian-Guthrie.com
Year of completion: 2013
No. of rooms: 7
Gross floor area/site area: 273 m²/3,740 m²
Luxury features: outdoor shower, fireplace

The building materials include polished concrete, natural timber and rendered masonry. The interior design is sparse and functional, offering everything one needs, but moving away from consumerist ideas of luxury and an abundance of possessions. Time spent outside is what matters here, the true luxury is the view and the wide open spaces, everything else is just secondary.

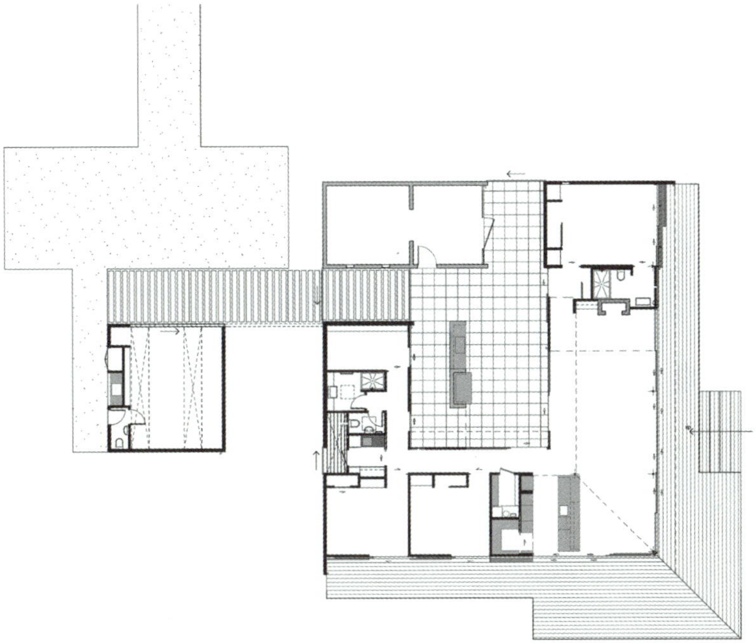

In Maori culture, a good pā represents power, effectiveness and prestige. A great inspiration for Mahia House.

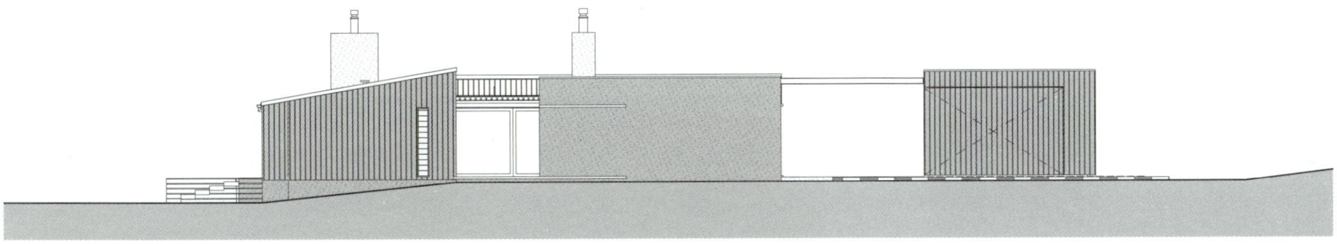

WHALE BEACH HOUSE
WHALE BEACH, AUSTRALIA

Facing north-east and located on a cliff edge, overlooking the Pacific Ocean, this new house enjoys stunning views but close neighbors. The client's brief asked for a family holiday home with a distinctly different feel to their city house which would embrace the concept of a relaxed beach pad. The plan comprises two wings, a private central courtyard and a terrace that extends towards the sea. This is the perfect place to relax, a small oasis with views that stretch uninterrupted for miles out towards the horizon. This layout maximizes the views from every room while overcoming the close proximity of the adjoining neighbors. From the street the building is deliberately understated to ensure privacy. Access is via the timber-clad central courtyard which conceals guest bedrooms and service rooms in an open arrangement. The splayed floor plan is evident from the courtyard as it opens to a projecting deck separating the living from the dining room.

Architect: Casey Brown Architecture
Interior designer: Casey Brown Architecture
Year of completion: 2008
No. of rooms: 10
Gross floor area/site area: 249 m²/561 m²
Luxury features: swimming pool

Enclosed in heavy stone walls, the lower level houses the master bedroom, study and ensuite, which open out to a pool and garden facing the ocean. The main materials include sandstone and thick vertical hardwood boarding; these were specifically chosen to suit the harsh environment.

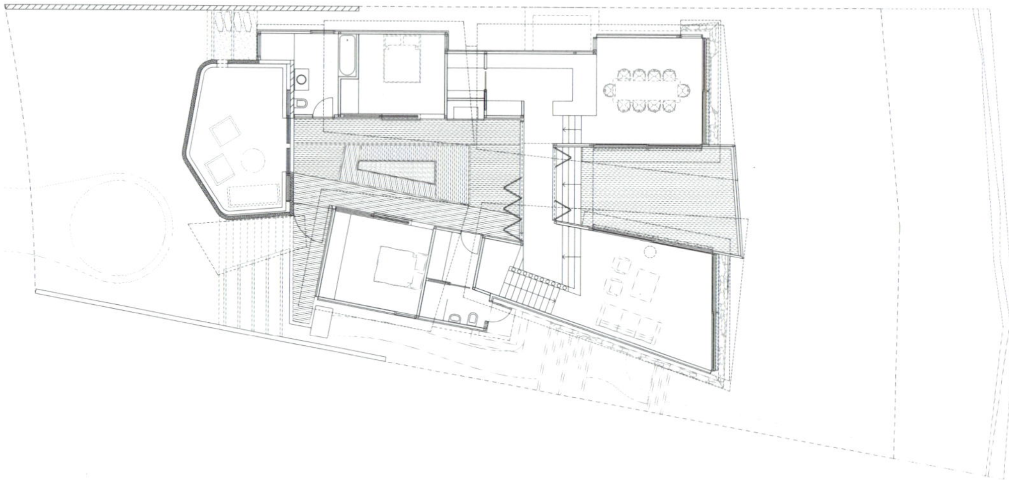

Stone, wood or glass? Why choose when you can have it all.

From the roadside, Cove House appears as a modest one-story home, while the side facing the coast steps down three stories, curving with the line of the shore and embracing the cove. The roof curves down to the north-east and rises up to the south creating a dynamic, light-filled space. The plan opens towards the view, north across Georgia Strait. At its highest point, the roof extends to cover an outdoor terrace. The top floor houses the entrance, main social spaces and terraces, while the bedrooms and private balconies are located on the middle floor. The lower floor houses the media and recreation room and storage space. A central staircase descends through the three stories and is linked to the roadside garden area and the beach. An exterior spiral stair connects the elevated terrace to the cove. The main material used is wood and this is continued inside the house, giving it a welcoming sense of continuity and harmony. The large windows and curving roof design give the house a unique appearance, successfully avoiding a beach house esthetic.

COVE HOUSE

DENMAN ISLAND, CANADA

Architect/designer: Blue Sky Architecture
Year of completion: 2011
No. of rooms: 15
Gross floor area/site area: 370 m²/1,560 m²

Inside, the large floor-to-ceiling windows make one feel the space larger than it is, a feeling that is emphasized by the panoramic views. Every aspect of this design has been developed with the view and the site in mind. The footprint has been kept to a minimum in order to cause as little damage as possible and natural materials have been used to complement the site.

The respect for nature of the Comox people, the native inhabitants of Denman Island, is mirrored in the house's natural design: back to the roots means back to the woods.

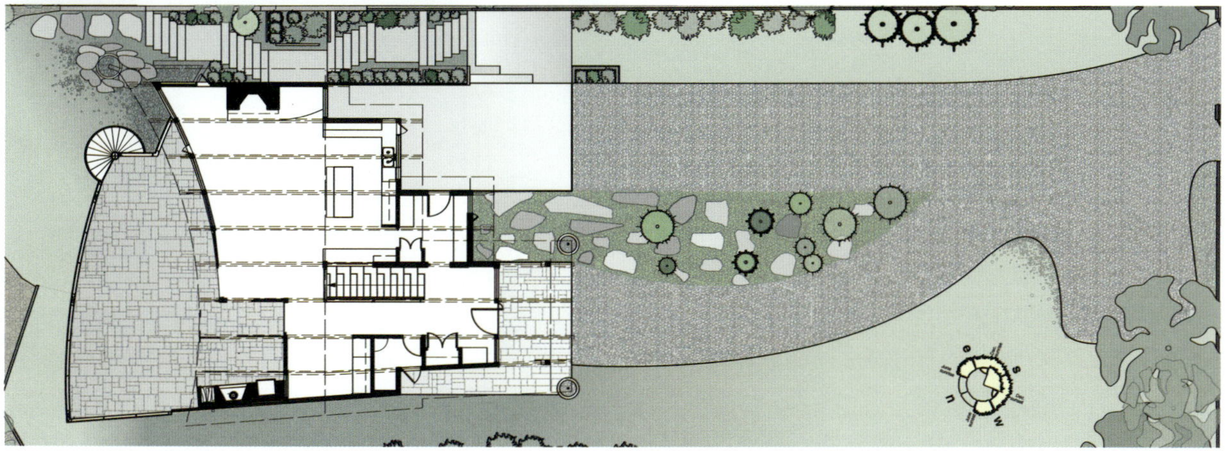

Waiheke, an idyllic island a 30-minute ferry ride from Auckland's downtown, is home to nearly 9,000 permanent residents alongside a holiday-making population whose weekend homes are scattered amongst the Island's sublime natural landscapes. The brief for this weekend property, set on a cliff edge with stunning gulf and vineyard outlooks, called for the accommodation of two families and a flexibility of use over time. A symmetrical composition of gables, based on a boathouse aesthetic, is formed around the central kitchen and living areas. This esthetic emphasizes a dialogue with the seaside setting, establishing a connection between the architecture itself and the wider context. Identical wings run parallel to the main gable form and accommodate the private spaces for each family. Each private wing can be closed off when not in use, making this house extremely flexible and adaptable, able to accommodate the family and guests.

WAIHEKE WEEKENDER
WAIHEKE ISLAND, NEW ZEALAND

Architect: Jason Bailey Limited
Interior designer: Anna Desbonnets
Year of completion: 2009
No. of rooms: 13
Gross floor area/site area: 290 m²/40,696 m²
Luxury features: wine cellar

The large terrace offers the perfect space to sit and relax, with views across the turquoise sea and out towards the other islands. The sloping steps leading away from the terrace also help to enhance the boathouse look. The living areas can be opened out if desired, making the terrace and the views essentially simply an extension of the living space. The living areas are flooded with light from the large windows, and this, combined with the high ceilings and the use of white and natural tones, also helps to emphasize a sense of space, making one feel the house large and accommodating.

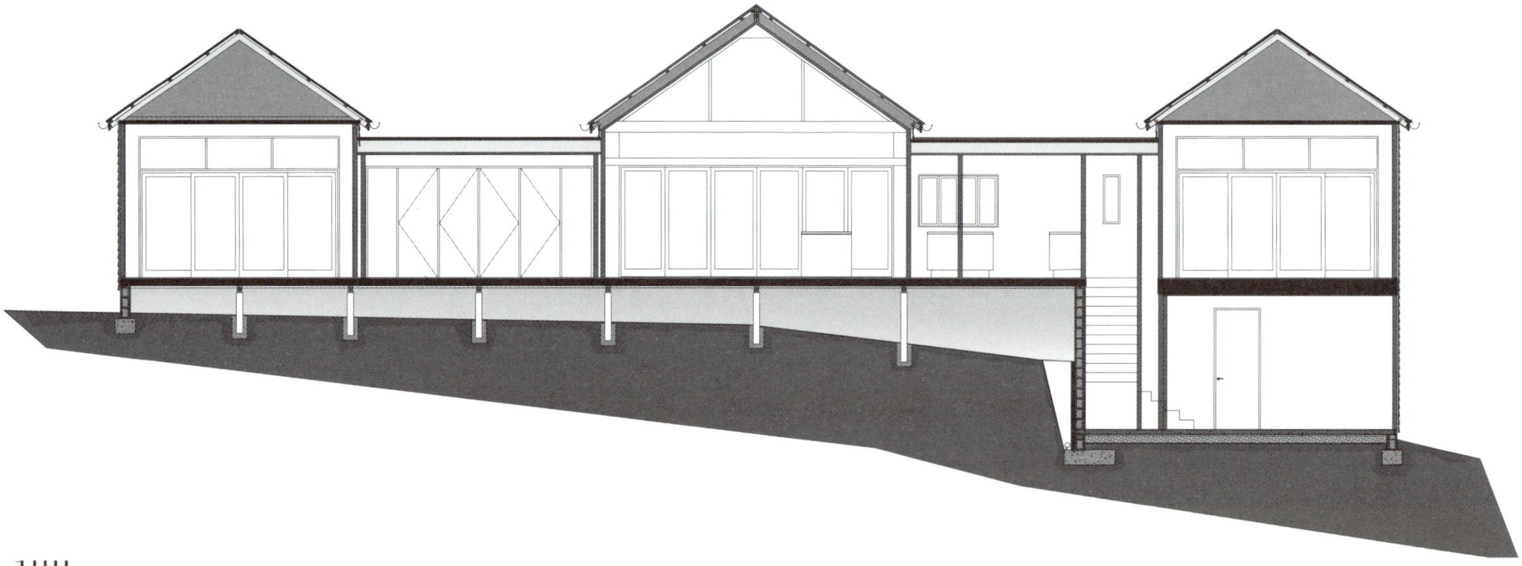

The boathouse esthetic is perfect for this setting, right next to the ocean.

An intriguing, yet private entrance to this home leads into a light-filled and transparent arrangement of living spaces with expansive views of Biscayne Bay and Downtown Miami. The home is located on the Venetian Islands, a string of exclusive man-made islands between Miami and Miami Beach. The south-facing residence is arranged around an elevated courtyard and employs various sun-shading strategies such as dynamic cantilevers and louvered balconies to adapt the home to its subtropical climate. The side of the house facing the bay is extremely open in character, with large windows reaching from the floor to the ceiling. In contrast, the front of the house is relatively closed, but with striking characteristics such as the double-height entrance and extensive smooth white surfaces. The home is raised several feet above the existing grade to better accommodate the occasional hurricane storm surge and also to confront the longer-term threat of sea level rise. Five bedrooms are located within the main house while another two-story guest suite is accessed via the courtyard and a louvered sky bridge.

SAN MARCO ISLAND RESIDENCE
MIAMI BEACH, FL, USA

Architect: [Strang] Architecture
Year of completion: 2014
No. of rooms: 12
Gross floor area/site area: 595 m²/975 m²
Luxury features: swimming pool, private beach, private jetty for boats

An open-plan living space on the ground floor provides direct access to the bay-front terrace, swimming pool and private dock. A spacious roof terrace allows for a 360-degree view of the tranquil islands of Biscayne Bay and the rapidly evolving skyline of Miami. The home has minimal material palette of white stucco, exposed concrete and oak flooring. The open-plan organization in combination with light and natural tones heightens the sense of space.

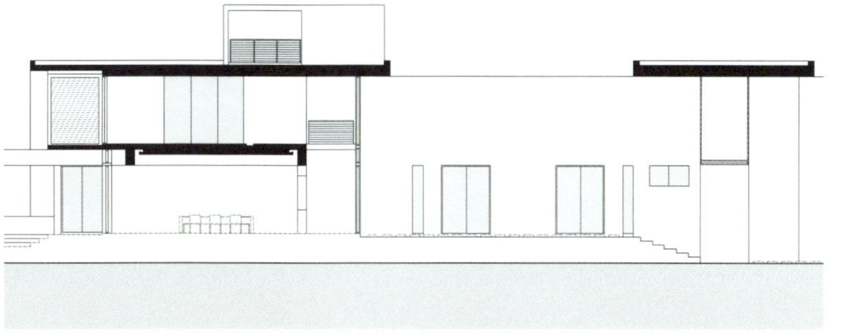

A glass edifice right on the ocean with waves lapping the balcony.

Bilgola Beach House is a family home that is relatively modest in size and restrained in terms of its material palette, yet rich in spatial experience and detail. The design ensures that the house is completely integrated into the spectacular site, located on one of Sydney's iconic beaches. The architectural form responds directly to the building's urban context, beachside location, orientation, environment and typography. The house is located high upon a ridge above Bilgola beach, overlooking the Pacific Ocean. Between the two street frontages, the architects inserted a split level building form: defensive and protective yet translucent to the north, and open, active and transparent to the south. The courtyard layout allows the house to act as an acoustic barrier to the busy northern road, while still enabling northern light to penetrate into the south facing living areas. The courtyard layout also allows an idea of a building section with a central split-level entry lobby, which addresses the northern and southern approaches equally and draws the occupants and visitors up to the main living areas.

BILGOLA RESIDENCE
BILGOLA BEACH, AUSTRALIA

Architect/designer: Tzannes
No. of rooms: 11
Gross floor area/site area: 296 m^2/1,715 m^2
Luxury features: outdoor swimming pool, hot tub, hydronic floor heating

The elevated living area offers spectacular views over the beach and the Pacific Ocean. It opens onto a covered balcony suspended above the swimming pool forming the southern wing of the building. The balcony and the deck below are designed to be bathed in northern sunlight in the winter, but sheltered and shaded in summer.

Where simplicity and luxury meet, is the perfect place to relax and unwind.

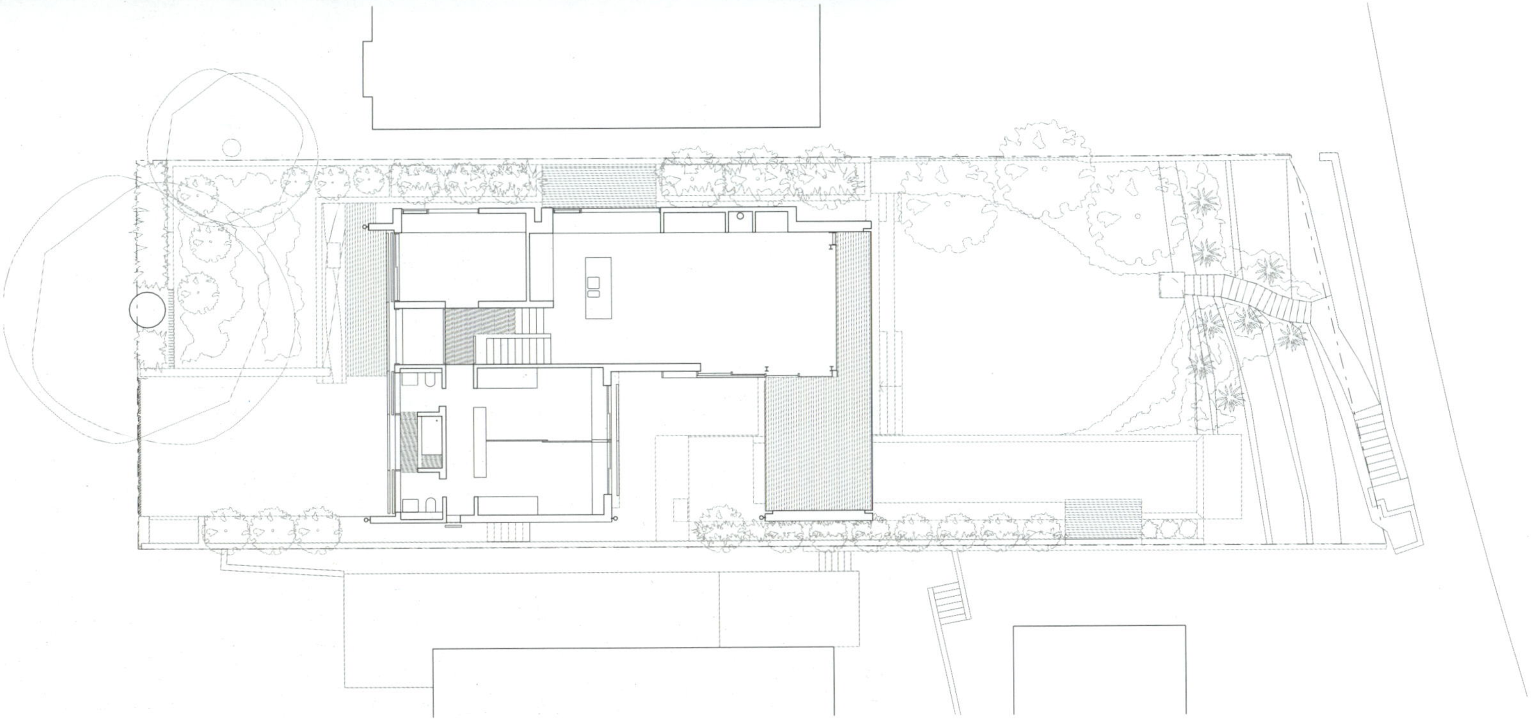

SOMJAI HOUSE
SURAT THANI, THAILAND

The house was designed as a retirement residence for the owner and, at the same time, is also intended to serve as a reception for Coco-NutNume resort where family, friends and guests can stop by and have a good time. The building comprises a main bedroom with bathrooms, a guest bedroom, a guest bathroom and a pantry for family cooking. The main hall building serves as a flexible multi-purpose space. It can be used as a living space, a party venue, coffee shop or even a yoga area. The upper deck was designed to provide panoramic views of the surrounding coconut plantation, the sea, Samui Island and the nearby hills.

The architecture relates to the skyline of hills behind the building which allows the wind to flow smoothly over the curving design. The front of the building was designed with an open angle to make the most of the view of the sea. The cantilever concept was used to protect the building from the hot sun. The main color used was red in order to provide a contrast to the green coconut plantation and the blue sea. Brick and polished concrete were selected as the main materials due to their cooling properties that help to protect the house from the heat.

Architect: NPDA studio | Nutthawut Piriyaprakob
Year of completion: 2015
No. of rooms: 7
Site area: 240 m²
Luxury features: private beach

The design plays with the contrast between open and closed areas, where brick and concrete walls are located directly next to open areas and glass windows. This gives the house a more playful appearance and breaks up its solidity. The thin iron staircase also shows the craftsmanship of local workmen.

Perfect for hot Thai summers: passive cooling!

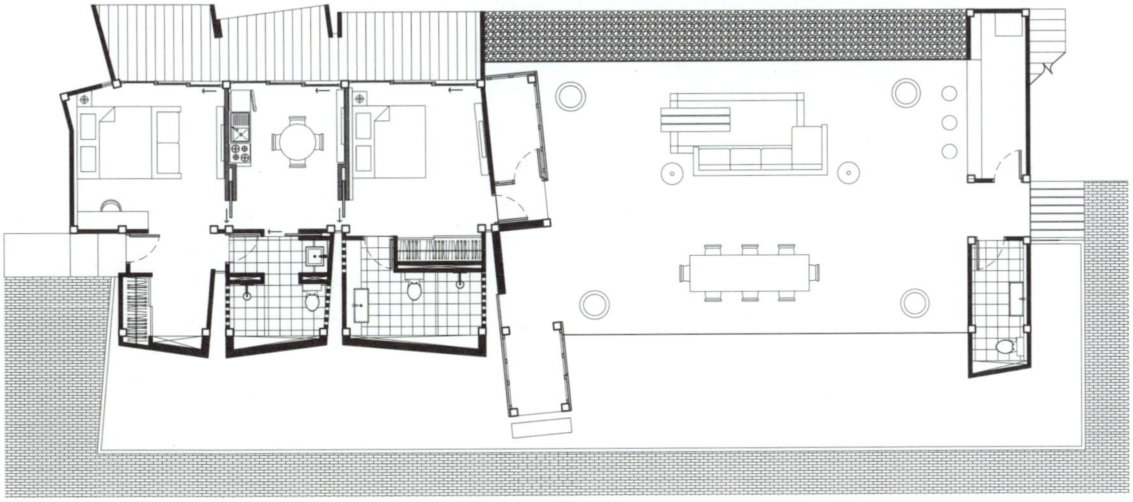

HUCKER RESIDENCE
MIAMI, FL, USA

Long, clean lines dominate the design of this waterfront compound in Miami's lush Coconut Grove neighborhood. The three-bedroom main house is located on a private canal with open water views of Biscayne Bay, while a secondary building contains a guest suite, office and art studio. The home was configured to take advantage of the prevailing southeasterly ocean breezes and views. A wrap-around planter, substituted in lieu of a guardrail, emphasizes the connection to the outdoors. Optimized for casual entertaining, the kitchen, dining and living area is immediately adjacent to a covered terrace. Both structures are raised substantially above the current grade to accommodate the threat of the occasional hurricane storm surge and rising sea levels. A lap pool, clad with Balinese stone tiles, and a small cabana are located within a beautifully landscaped garden. Generous overhangs offer protection from Florida's harsh climate while providing the home with its unique esthetic.

Architect: [Strang] Architecture
Year of completion: 2015
No. of rooms: 10
Gross floor area/site area: 697 m^2/1,212 m^2
Luxury features: swimming pool, private beach, private jetty

Louvers are used to further adapt the design to its subtropical climate. Inside, the palette comprises largely light and natural tones, these create a strong contrast to the lush green foliage surrounding the house and also add to the natural 'feel' of the design. The open-plan arrangement also gives a sense of infinite space, with most rooms offering views out over the water.

The contemporary idea of living in the Garden of Eden.

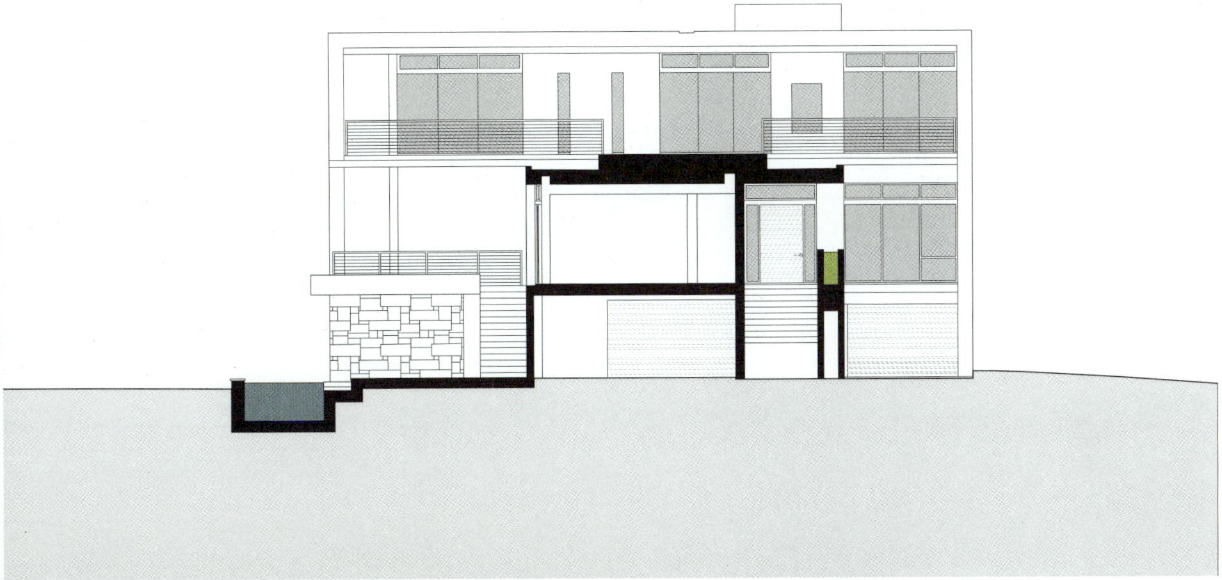

This house is located on a clifftop site in a gated community in Playa Misterio, 117 kilometers south of Lima. The design is a clever solution to specific program requirements demanded by the client, a successful surgeon with a large family. The social area is located next to the entrance and occupies two levels. The accommodation for children and parents was organized into two parts. The swimming pool and recreational facilities are also located on the lower levels, occupying a series of terraces designed to connect the house with the ocean. The house is strikingly modern both inside and out. The angular, staggered design of the exterior is repeated inside the house, where bold colors such as green, blue and red highlight specific areas. From the outside, the house has both white and gray areas, which helps it blend in with the cliff.

ALVAREZ BEACH HOUSE
PLAYA MISTERIO, PERU

Architect/designer: Longhi Architects
Year of completion: 2010
No. of rooms: 9
Gross floor area/site area: 580 m^2/700 m^2
Luxury features: swimming pool, private beach, terraces on each level, private bar

A highlight of the design are the terraces on each level. This not only establishes a strong connection between interior and exterior, it also mimics the jutting rocky outcrops of the nearby cliffs and strengthens the spatial connection between the house and the ocean. The house is oriented towards the ocean, which not only makes the most of the views but also offers more privacy, as the side facing the beach is open, while the side facing the road is protected from the gaze of passersby.

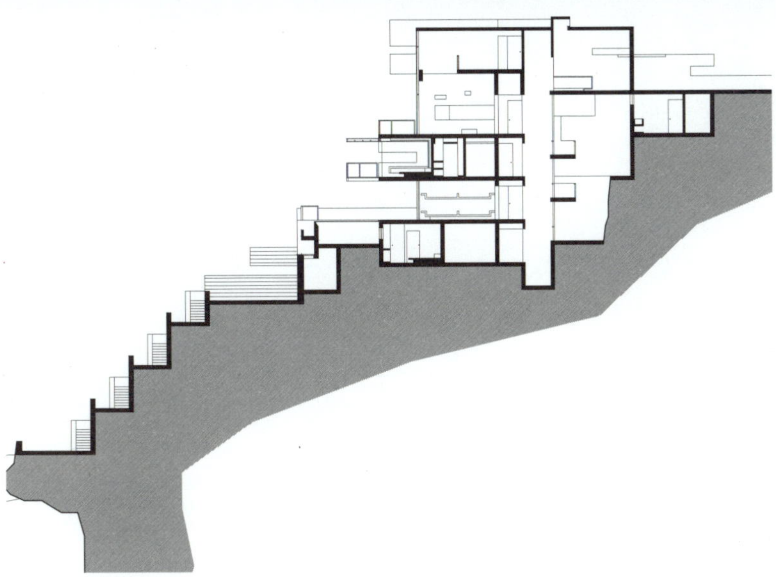

10

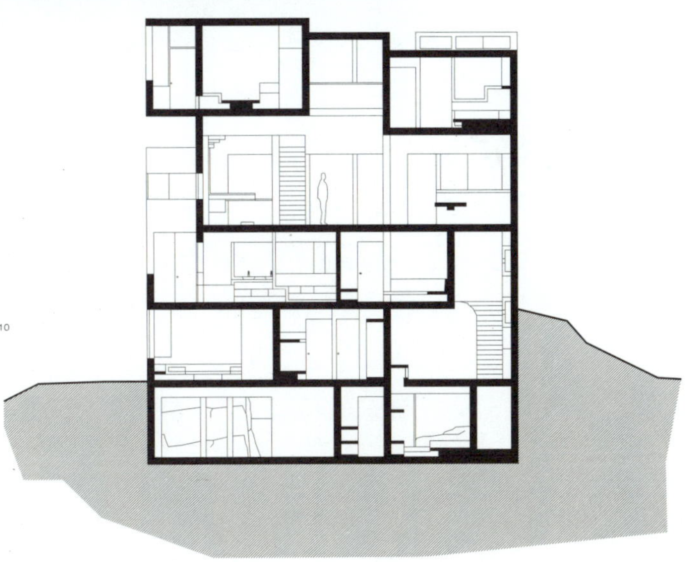

This design makes the most of the sloping site, transforming it into a design feature rather than allowing it to act as a limitation.

Lavaflow 5 frames the sea and sky with structure and lines. The slender steel frame supports walls of varying opacity; from nothing, to glass, to screen, to solid – creating a laminate of materials tempering the expansive view overlooking the Hamakua coastline on Hawaii's Big Island. The remoteness of the site, the desire for large open expanses and a commitment to use sustainable building techniques led the architect to investigate prefabrication in steel as a method of construction. The house is long and thin with all rooms facing north towards the ocean. Circulation is on the south side and sunlight is mitigated along this extended hall with an epoxy resin screen – a product usually used for industrial decking. The house is elevated above the site and entered across a large reflecting pond. The hilltop site makes the most of sweeping views of the ocean. The narrow plan of the house provides passive cooling through cross ventilation allowing for the elimination of mechanical air conditioning.

LAVAFLOW 5
HAMAKUA COAST, HAWAII, USA

Architect: Craig Steely Architecture
Year of completion: 2013
No. of rooms: 10
Gross floor area/site area: 260 m²/121,406 m²
Luxury features: pond

The industrial screen filters the sunlight creating a consistent and diffused interior light quality throughout the day. Another sustainable feature includes a solar heating system for domestic hot water. This decidedly simple building of steel, concrete and glass provides the essential requirements for living while focusing on living experientially in Hawaii's dynamic environment.

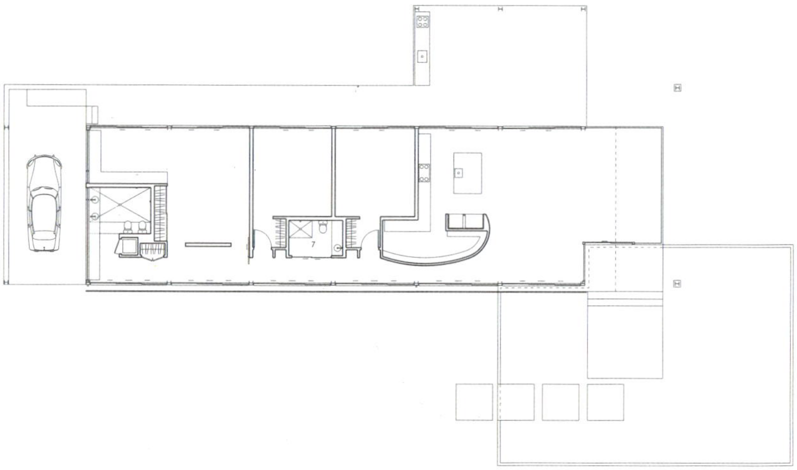

Industrial revolution reinterpreted in the 'Aloha State', Hawaii's official byname.

The most striking feature of this house is its open structure with large expanses of glass, and the long swimming pool running along the site and positioned parallel to the coast. The front of the house faces the ocean and is largely glazed, with a few supporting pillars bearing the weight of the upper floor. The pillars are positioned rather randomly as opposed to being built in a strict grid. This gives the interior a more relaxed and unusual character and means that they can be positioned to interrupt the view as little as possible. The interior is open-plan, with large open rooms where the light can flow through uninterrupted by unnecessary walls. The natural tones and colors also add to a sense of never-ending, flowing space. The design of the staircase also reflects this, with a wide-sweeping flight of stairs sloping gracefully upwards, rather than a more traditional, narrow closed in stairway. The stairwell also forms a void through the house, a large circular atrium that helps to make the stairs a central feature of the design.

VERONICA BEACH HOUSE
PLAYA POSEIDÓN, PERU

Architect: Longhi Architects
Year of completion: 2014
No. of rooms: 8
Gross floor area/site area: 650 m²/545 m²
Luxury features: swimming pool, private bar

From the outside, the house appears almost like a ship sailing off towards the horizon. The wooden decks and large windows also help to emphasize this.

Here, even the rock face is integrated into the modern interior design.

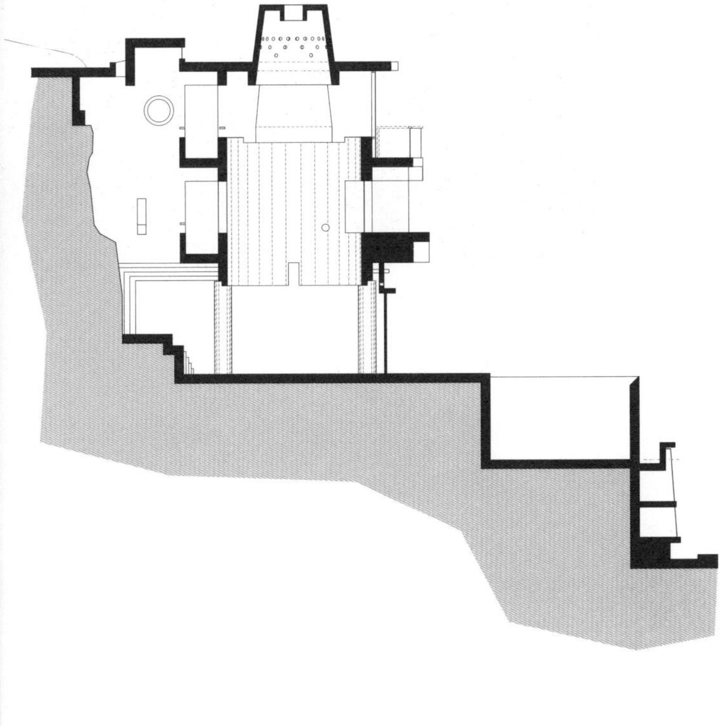

The client's brief was to create a six-bedroom dream villa on a prime plot of land on the west coast of Phang Nga province at the southern end of Thailand. The house was to be open and spacious with extensive decks, terraces and lawns and specifically designed so that it would be ideal for two families visiting at the same time. Aside from the spectacular view, an added element was to be a 25-meter swimming pool that has now become one of the principal features around which the house is laid out. The main living area is positioned at one end of the pool and can be completely opened up, allowing the almost constant monsoon breeze to cool the space and draw air from the other rooms into the house. The overriding concept involved the creation of a dynamic, contemporary vacation home that is a world apart from city life. The main entrance is through this space and access to all areas of the home, whether indoors or out, is via this pivotal area.

SAVA SAI
PHANG NGA, THAILAND

Architect: Original Vision Limited
Year of completion: 2010
No. of rooms: 14
Gross floor area/site area: 760 m²/1,448 m²
Luxury features: swimming pool, private beach

The client's desire for a dynamic, contemporary, tropical villa that feels open and exciting has been fulfilled in a composition that embraces the local climate and a free and easy vacation lifestyle. Water also plays a significant role with a reflection pond at the entrance continuing as the major swimming pool element on the other side of the living space.

The large wooden terrace almost gives the feeling of living on a raft, as if you could cast off at any moment.

On a rocky granite cliff overlooking the Atlantic Ocean near Ketch Harbour, Nova Scotia, this house is a series of angled glass and raw concrete pavilions that capture the dramatic landscape in every direction. Crowned by gently curving zinc roofs, each pavilion frames views of a historic lighthouse, the sea lanes to Halifax and a World War II allied bunker. The entrance to the house is subtle; the driveway is faced with the austere concrete wall of the rear façade, so that only upon entering the home beneath an undulating canopy does one discover the layout of the house and view from within. Set along a linear entry hallway, the pavilions also define programmatic areas, with the den, living/dining rooms, the kitchen and master bedroom each ensconced in their own space. Two additional bedrooms on the second level cantilever off the main body of the house, further enhancing the experience of the site. The house is set on landscaped terraces that provide a platform for lounging areas that open up to the views, with long outdoor patios which recall the deck of an ocean-going ship.

NOVA SCOTIA HOUSE
KETCH HARBOUR, CANADA

Architect: Alexander Gorlin Architects
Year of completion: 2012
No. of rooms: 8
Gross floor area/site area: 465 m²/202,343 m²

The wild rocks and crashing waves are as sublime a site as any in the world, and the house is a perfect balance between architecture and nature. The large volume is afforded a strikingly lightweight appearance thanks to the extensive use of glass. This of course also has the added advantage of drawing a wealth of light inside and giving the house a bright and welcoming appearance.

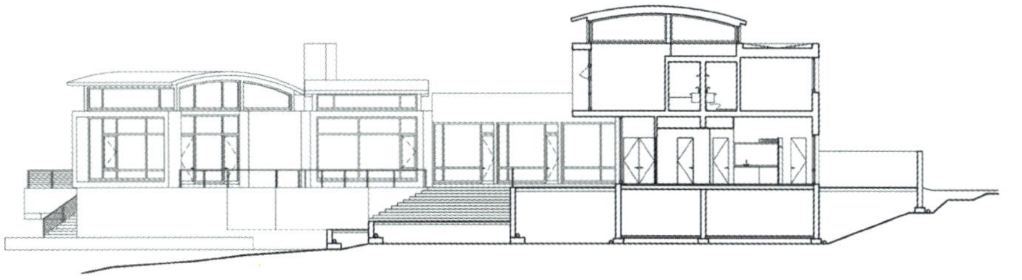

I am a rock: camouflage at its best.

ATREVIDA HOUSE
PUERTO JIMENEZ, COSTA RICA

Designed for a Corsican family that comes here every year to surf, this house is located on a site with prevailing sandy soil and covered with lush tropical foliage. The design of the house is bold and its open character gives residents the desired sense of freedom. Built by using Guadua bamboo, the house is two stories in height and designed to withstand earthquakes. It has been built on a high concrete base, which helps to protect and isolate the bamboo from water. The design cleverly encourages cross ventilation, while the open areas and large windows have the additional advantage of drawing a wealth of light inside. A system on the roof provides energy for heating water, reinforcing the eco-friendly character of the entire design. The house clearly responds to its surroundings: The wide wooden supports, the use of bamboo and wood, the openness of the ground floor in contrast to the more solid second floor all deliberately evoke the idea of a group of trees in a forest.

Architect: Luz de Piedra
Interior designer: Luz De Piedra
Furniture designer: Stagno Melendez Letelier
Year of completion: 2011
No. of rooms: 5
Gross floor area/site area: 300 m²/1,600 m²
Luxury features: swimming pool

The house responds to the site, welcoming nature rather than attempting to shut it out. Inside, the high ceilings and white walls give a sense of space, so that one never feels confined, even when spending time indoors. Bamboo is present throughout and this reflects artisan building techniques, providing the flexibility needed for such a structure, but combined with modern materials such as concrete to give the design a modern appearance.

Bamboo and concrete — tradition meets modernity.

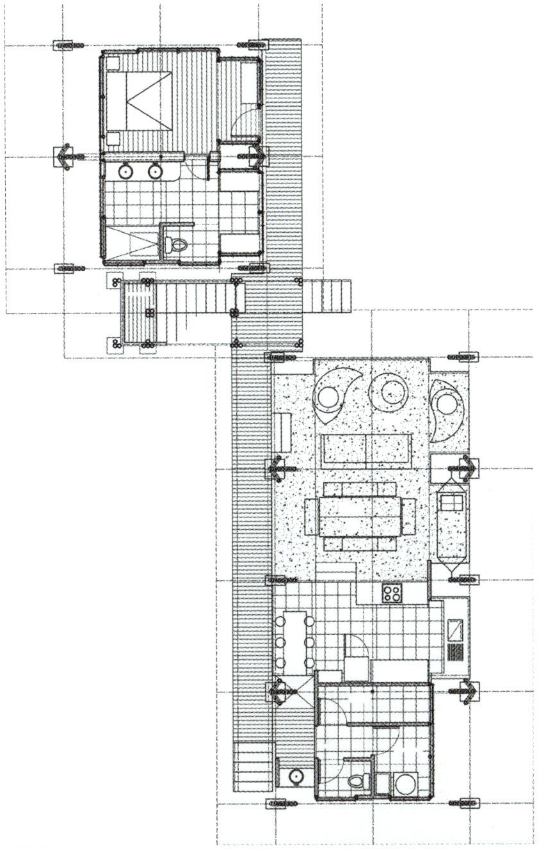

INDEX

PICTURE CREDITS

Peter Aaron/OTTO 182–185
Anotherspacestudio & Jirasak Thongyuak 154–157
Steve Back 150–153
Benjamin Benschneider 80–83
Patrick Bingham-Hall 134–137
Blue Sky Architecture 140 b.
Brett Boardman 49 a. l.
Jerritt Boomer 138, 139 b., 140 a. l., 141
Géraldine Bruneel 61 r., 62 a., 63 b.
Bruce Buck 147 a., 148 b. r., 149 b. r.
Matthew Carbone 30–41
Nils Petter Dale 96–101
Bruce Damonte 122–125, 168–171
Filip Dujardin 20–23
Christine Francis, Melbourne 56–59
Murray Fredericks 114–117
Amit Geron (photographic styling by Eti Buskila) 84–87
Francesca Giovanelli 102–105
Jesús Granada 8–11
José Hevia 52–55
Aryeh Kornfeld 68–71
Javier Larrea 118–121
Robert Les 42–47
Adam Letch 72–75, 88–91
Andrew Loiterton 178–181
Kallan Macleod 142–145
Marcos Mendizabal 76–79
Mads Mogensen 110–113
Peter Powles 139 a.
Sergio Pucci 186–189
Patrick Reynolds 24–29, 126–133
Ieva Saudargaite 60, 61 l., 62 b.
Juan Solano 64–67, 162–167 , 172–177
Ed Sozinho 107 a., 108, 109
Graham Syed 106, 107 b.
Brett Turner 92–95
Claudia Uribe 146 l., 148 b. l., 148 a. r; 158–161
Simon Whitbread 48, 49 a. r., 50, 51
Calder Wilson 147 b.

All other pictures were made available by the architects and /or designers.